CHINA

SECRETS OF THE DRAGON

Published by
Kandour Limited
Monticello House
45 Russell Square
London WC1B 4JP
United Kingdom

First published 2007

10 9 8 7 6 5 4 3 2 1

Managing Editor: Ruth Urbom

Editorial Assistant: Emma Agyemang

Creative Director: Alexander Rose

Jacket Design: Alex Ingr

Design Layout: Daniel Oliver

Art Editor: David Fraser

Production Manager: Carol Titchener

Sales & Editorial Manager: Karen Lomax

Author: Samantha Austin

Additional Material: Kaspa Hazlewood

Printed and bound in Singapore

ISBN 13: 978-1-905741-44-1

A catalogue record of this book is available from the British Library

CHINA

SECRETS OF THE DRAGON

SAMANTHA AUSTIN

k

Kandour Ltd

Contents

Introduction

China is a country only slightly smaller than the whole of North America and boasts diverse terrain, a myriad of cultures and customs, and a richly complex history.

China is often depicted in the West as a country shrouded in intrigue and mystery. As a nation often viewed as the epitome of the "Far East," China is typically imagined through such iconic images as dragons, red lanterns, the face of Mao Zedong, or the tranquil seated pose of the Buddha, to name but a few. But China—a country only slightly smaller than North America, covering 3.7 million square miles (9.6 million sq km)—is a country with diverse terrain, a myriad of cultures and customs, and a richly complex history. Many will argue that it is quickly asserting itself in this century's race to become a new political and economic superpower.

In addition to China's dramatic rise in population within the last century and a half—which saw its population increase by over 900 million to its current total of over 1.3 billion—China has undergone substantial and radical transformations as a nation. It has seen the collapse of empires ruled by a succession of dynasties which were markedly different from one era of rule to the next, the introduction of the People's Republic of China (PRC) in 1949, the opening of its doors to the West and the consequent rapid push for modernization, not to mention the considerable effect that all of these changes have had on the people and cultures of China.

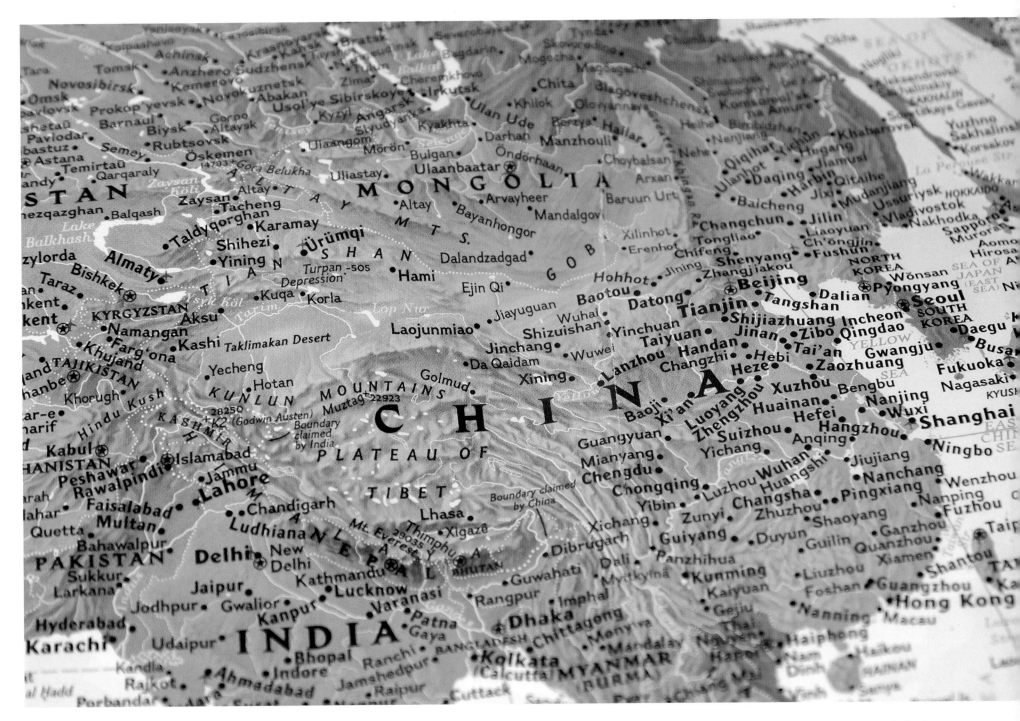

Indeed, China can never mean just one thing at any given time. If there is one image that China conjures up, it is one of change. Like the mythical beast that so many conflate with this dynamic country, the dragon embodies oppositions of change that China has seen and continues to confront. It is both a real and an imaginary animal, with the body of a winged reptile but with fire-breathing powers that no living creature possesses. In this sense, the

Left: *Perhaps China's most important symbol, the dragon is present in all aspects of Chinese society and history.*

Above: *China is one of the world's largest countries in size and boasts the world's largest population.*

dragon belongs to the past, and the present as well as the future. As an icon of the past, it is viewed as mythological and belongs to creation stories of old. Today, the dragon continues to be a contemporary image and metaphor for China. Yet, because the dragon holds no real place within the animal kingdom but maintains powers that secure its place among the most supreme and evolved beings, it can be associated with the future. And, like the dragon, China moves with great speed and agility toward the future, all the while keeping a scaly claw firmly clasped to the place from which it came.

Today, more people are visiting China than ever before. The psychological distance that once placed China at the far end of the earth is quickly being replaced by a notion of China as an accessible (albeit still "exotic") destination. As the host of the 2008 Summer Olympics, China's capital of Beijing has been focused on the task of what the PRC refers to as modernization. Neighborhoods, referred to as *hutong* in Mandarin, the official spoken language of China, are being replaced with new high-rise buildings and shopping centers at a dizzying speed. While many people, both inside China as well as outside, praise the economic development and rapid urbanization that is taking place, there is also another side to the developmental coin, so to speak, that includes extreme environmental degradation and further exploitation of migrant workers who come to the big cities looking for a new prosperous future. This, in turn, has led to increasing crime rates and reduced financial opportunity, many claim. As with any country under such pressures of change, the sword is double-sided. For some, the modernization project offers huge opportunity, financial security and freedom from rigid rules and practices of the "old" China. However, for others, modernization means leaving one's hometown for the prospect of work in an urban setting, competing for

As a response to the increasing number of tourists, China is catering more and more to a Western clientele. Large American corporations, like Starbucks, McDonald's and Pizza Hut are rapidly gaining popularity.

Left: *Auspicious signs declaring good luck and health are a common sight on doorways throughout China.*

Below: *The Flag of the People's Republic of China.*

9

Above: *The Great Wall of China stretches over several provinces and covers thousands of miles.*

Right: *Qin Shi Huangdi's Terracotta Army is one of China's most popular tourist attractions.*

jobs that often entail exploitative and possibly physically dangerous working conditions, and even witnessing the destruction of the *hutong* that their family has lived in for generations to make way for concrete apartment buildings. If anything is certain about China's modernization project, it is that it is a highly contested and complex process affecting its population in varying ways.

Yet what can explain the dramatic increase in tourism within China's borders? While some may argue that it is precisely the PRC's focus on modernization projects, especially in such major cities as Beijing, Shanghai and Chongqing, others may opt for a more subtle reason.

It could be argued that the China of today as compared to the China of the 1950s, '60s, and even '70s is beyond comparison, evidenced by the increasing ubiquity of western-style shopping centers and luxury hotels, but step a little outside the borders of these cities and a much different China emerges. Deng Xiaoping's "reform and opening" policy toward Western countries over twenty years ago opened the door for tourists to visit China once again. As a response to the increasing number of visitors, China is catering more and more to a Western clientele. Large American corporations, like Starbucks, McDonald's and Pizza Hut, continue to gain in popularity not just in major Chinese urban centers like Beijing and Shanghai, but in smaller or mid-sized cities as well. Western movies, music, food, fashion and even religion are gaining more and more currency within China's borders making, for some travelers, an easier visit and, for others, disappointing and disturbing proof of globalization.

Up until the mid-twentieth century, China saw much continuity between its rural and urban centers. Historically, there had not been such a great divide between town and country, as

the economic and administrative centers often overlapped and merged. Villages were set up in surrounding circles, creating continuous communities with various market centers. Western encroachment in China after the Opium Wars, however, changed the traditional model of market towns and villages. As a result of various economic and social policies such as the expansion and development of cities like Shanghai in the 1920s and the household registration system of the 1950s, the divide between country and city began to become more and more distinct. During the 1940s and '50s, the city was viewed as a parasitic influence on China, representing Western bourgeois tendencies that were denounced by the Communists under Mao. For Mao, the future of China was to be found in the countryside. During the Great Leap Forward, Mao's economic and social reform plan of the late 1950s, he sent thousands of Chinese citizens to the countryside to be "re-educated." Much has changed since then, especially since Deng Xiaoping's efforts and policies directed toward opening the doors between China and the West.

Today, the vast majority of China's 1.3 billion citizens still reside in rural areas. The confluence between rural and urban is becoming more and more common to the landscape of China, as cities sprawl outward more and more toward what was once farming land and small villages. If the divide between rural China and urban China was once large, the countryside is seeing perhaps more fluidity than ever before between these two important landscapes.

The geography and terrain of China alone proves that it is a place of grand, large-scale contrast. Home to the second-lowest area in the world—the Turpan Depression, sitting 505 feet below sea level—and the highest peak in the world—Mount Everest rising to 29,029 feet (8850 m)—China is a land of extremes. Snaking through this vast terrain stands the Great Wall of China, whose exact length remains under dispute, but estimates vary anywhere between 1,500 miles to 4,000 miles long. Though the wall is not a continuous structure but more like a series of walls, forts and earthen ramparts, what we consider the Great Wall of China stretches from the western province of Qinghai all the way to its most recently built segments just outside Beijing. It indeed is a feat of enormous human achievement and remains a symbol of China's fragility and tenacity throughout history.

Indeed, China is a land of contrasts. This contrast has certainly fueled the curiosity of outside travelers, who want to confirm the images they see throughout the media with their own eyes. The juxtaposition of a dynastic, ancient or communist China of Mao's time with a China that is fixated on the future has created a dramatic polarity. The fusion of past with future to give way to a present filled with the images and icons of both eras—that which has been and that which is to come—is what fascinates and allures many to China. In Beijing alone, one can view skyscrapers along side the remnants of the ancient city walls, nearly 1,000 years old.

As one of the longest unified civilizations in the world, the history of China is no simple matter. Distinguished by dynastic rule—eras punctuated with warfare and shifts in power—China's long and continuous history is as much about expansion and assimilation as it is about continuity and cohesion. For, in order that China survive through eras of struggle and resistance all the while maintaining its language and culture, the country has had to adapt again and again over its several thousand-year history.

China is a major center for archaeology and forensic anthropology, with discoveries such as the Terracotta Warriors in the ancient

Left: *More than any other color, red symbolizes the nation and people of China.*

Below: *One of China's central religions, Buddhism is practiced by millions across the country.*

Because the Chinese language does not contain an alphabet, learning to read involves memorizing each word with its corresponding character.

Below: *The unmistakable Hong Kong skyline.*

Right: *The tranquil Li River near the southern city of Guilin.*

capitol of Xi'an as evidence of the abundant artifacts found hidden underneath Chinese soil. Today, many Chinese both within China and outside it refer to themselves as Han Chinese. This term refers to the Han dynasty, which ran from 206 BC–AD 220 and is known as the "golden age" of Chinese history. The Chinese government officially recognizes 56 ethnic minorities (including the Han, which is the largest group accounting for over 92% of China's population). Each of these groups, which together account for 8% of the Chinese population, has its own distinct culture, customs, and language. Contrary to popular images of China's people as a homogenous group, diversity can be found in all of its 23 provinces. Furthermore, even within the 92% Han majority, distinct differences—particularly in food and language—can be found.

Though Mandarin—referred to as *Putonghua*, meaning literally "national spoken language"— is the official language of China, there are many regional dialects and five distinctly different regional versions of spoken Chinese. The written language of Mandarin Chinese finds its roots in the Sino-Tibetan family of languages and is based on symbols used to represent objects or ideas. This system has remained remarkably consistent since its inception during the Shang dynasty (16th–11th centuries BC). Because the Chinese language does not contain an alphabet, learning to read involves memorizing each word with its corresponding character. Some estimate that it takes a knowledge of between 3,000 and 4,000 characters to read a newspaper alone. UNESCO estimates that China has the second-largest illiterate population after India, with a literacy rate of around 85%. While written Chinese is standard among all regions within China, spoken Chinese varies and contains many regional dialects. Four distinct tones define spoken words that, without the use of the correct corresponding tone for each one,

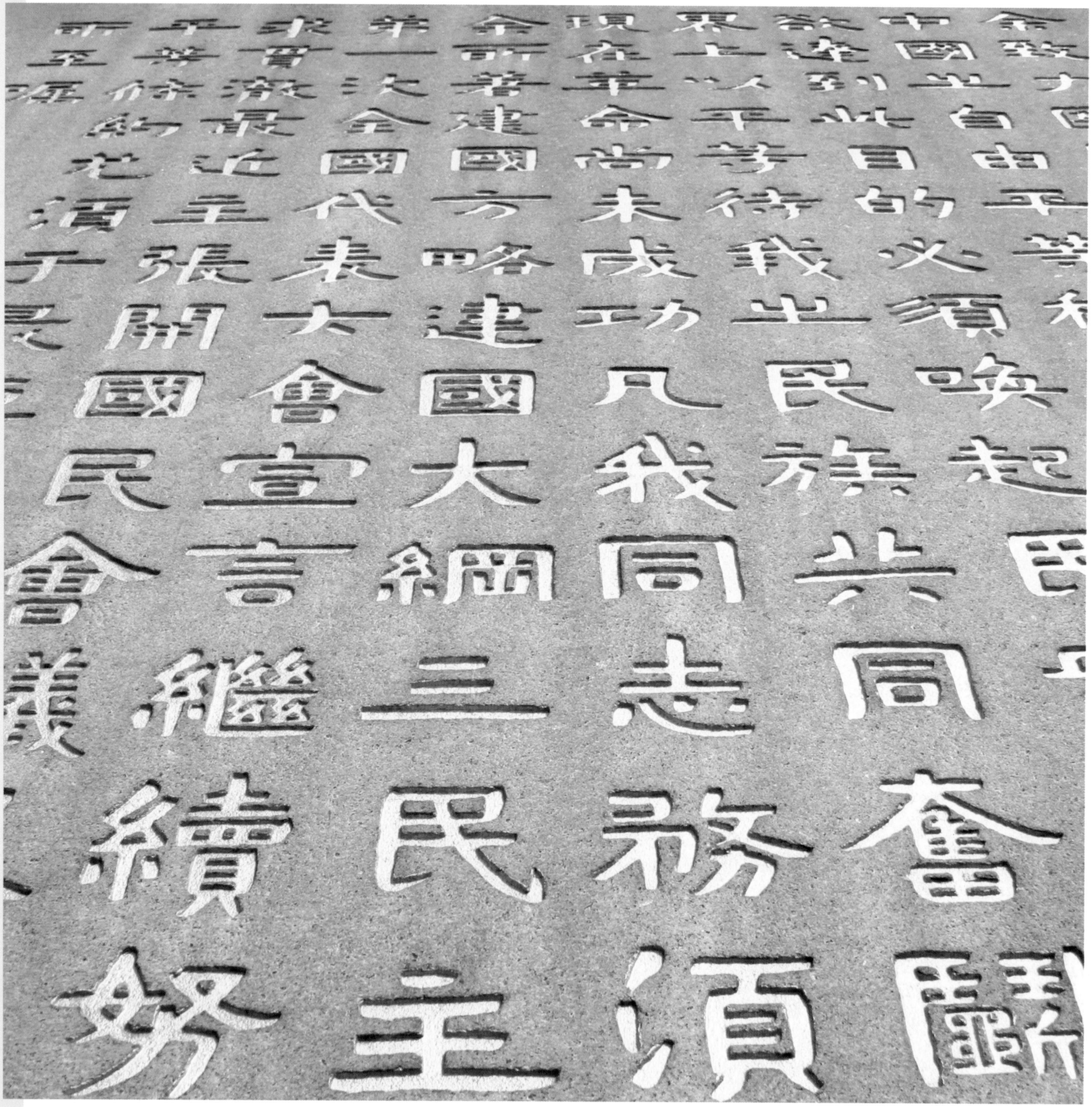

would sound exactly the same. Unless educated in standard spoken Mandarin, it would not be an unlikely scenario for someone from Sichuan and someone from Shanghai to have difficulty communicating with each other because of regional variations in vocabulary and grammar. Cantonese, which is spoken in southern China in areas including Hong Kong and Guangdong, is considered a completely different language from Mandarin Chinese.

Like language, food changes from province to province. Sichuan-style cuisine, which is perhaps the best-known Chinese cuisine outside China, is renowned for its extremely spicy and saucy flavors, whereas southern Chinese cuisine tends to focus on subtlety of flavors. Yet, while cuisine style and content vary all over the country, food has been and continues to be a unifying force among the people of China. Rice, considered the center of any meal, is vital to the tradition of Chinese food and to the importance placed on the ritual and event of eating within Chinese culture. Food is immensely important within China and, as any visitor to China will tell you, is a key (if not *the* central) experience to understanding Chinese culture.

As with most facets of Chinese life, religion and the arts have changed along with the economic and political turmoil witnessed by China over the past century and a half. The religious practices of China have gone through everything from mass denunciation of "traditional" ways and practices during the Cultural Revolution to a slow revival of religion as a viable outlet for the daily bureaucratic rigidity that many within China face. Like religion, many art forms were banned during the early days of communist rule. The Beijing Opera is but one example of an art form that was forbidden during the Cultural Revolution, yet it has survived and remains a huge attraction for foreign tourists and Chinese alike. Today, the visual arts of China fill contemporary art galleries and museums,

While cuisine style and content vary all over the country, food has been and continues to be a unifying force among the people of China.

Left: *The Chinese language consists of thousands of characters, each unique in meaning.*

Below: *Bamboo grows in abundance throughout southern China and is used for a variety of purposes, ranging from scaffolding to birdcages.*

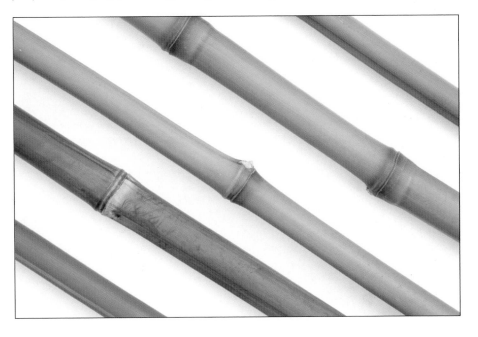

While communism during the Mao era had horrific consequences for the peasants of rural China, it also had a positive effect on the lives and roles of women in China.

Below: *The image of the setting sun over one of China's major cities.*

Right: *Mao remains a strong cultural and historical icon of China's turbulent past.*

generating what many art critics consider to be an unprecedented and exciting path unparalleled in modern art. Galleries, like the Red Gate Gallery of Beijing, display works by artists who are known for their critical depiction of China's past, present, and rapid movement toward the future.

Along with changes in the arts and religion, China has seen traditional roles within the family and society at large change alongside the political and economic transformations the country has undergone during the 20th century. Travel to a small village, however, and it is not unlikely to see the bound feet of the elderly women of the village—a reminder of the not-so-distant past where practices like this were remarkably common. While foot binding is now an image linked with China's past, it would be inaccurate to claim that women in today's China no longer face sexism, violence, or unequal status. It may be argued that while communism during the Mao era had horrific consequences for the peasants of rural China, it also had a positive effect on the lives and roles of women in China. While it is true that, by and large, more opportunities in education and employment exist today for the women of China, differences between Han Chinese women and minority women and between women who live in rural China versus those who live in major cities cannot be overlooked. The One Child Policy, developed in 1979 to curb explosive population growth, has been received with much controversy and speculation as to its effects on the health of women and children within China.

Despite the rapid rate of change in China, visitors to China during Spring Festival—the 6–8 weeks surrounding the Chinese New Year, typically falling sometime in late January or early February—can easily see how the rituals and festivals that have been in place for thousands of years continue to flourish and bring joy to people's lives. The Chinese New Year is unarguably the most important time of year for Chinese people of all ages. According to the lunar calendar, the New Year begins on the day of the first new moon after January 21. It is a time when families gather together to celebrate, exchange gifts, cook traditional foods such as *jiaozi* (dumplings), and decorate their doors with vibrant red posters declaring good fortune in the year to come. In the Chinese Zodiac, which is associated with the New Year, each year is associated with an animal of the 12-year zodiac cycle. Each person born within a particular year is thought to embody the characteristics of the animal for that year. The matching of signs becomes especially important in marriage proposals. Other important festivals include Mid-Autumn Festival, Dragon Boat Festival, Lantern Festival and Grave-Sweeping Festival. These festivals, each with its own practice and accompanying legend, all involve the bringing about of good fortune and prosperity.

Complex, grand, diverse, changing—these are but a few of the words that come to mind when thinking of China. Representing the Chinese nation as well as the emperor, the dragon continues to be a symbol of luck, prosperity, and protection to the people of China. Will people's relationship to this symbol change as China continues to transform itself? It may be that, of all the remnants of China's past, the dragon will endure precisely because it is also a symbol for change and transformation. Like the snake, it can shed its skin again and again, so the dragon incorporates change into its very being. The following chapters take this notion in mind as they explore four major Chinese cities—Xi'an, Beijing, Shanghai, and Hong Kong—and follow, like the tail of a dragon, the movement of the historical and cultural centers of China. No single city can possibly encompass all of a country. Yet, each of these cities has, in its own way, made pivotal contributions to all aspects of Chinese culture and society.

Xi'an

Xi'an region was a center of early Chinese culture and society. Settlements in what we know today as Xi'an date back to the Neolithic period, as dramatic archeological remains have proven.

The capital of present-day Shaanxi province, the area just outside of modern Xi'an was established as the ancient capital of China during the Zhou dynasty (1100–256 BC) in 1066 BC. Termed Chang'an, meaning "Enduring Peace," during the Tang dynasty (618–907 AD), this region had long since been a center of early Chinese culture and society. Settlements in what we know today as Xi'an date back to the Neolithic period, as archeological remains have proven. Xi'an was the capital for nearly 1,200 years, serving a remarkable 11 dynasties. Some estimate that it was during the Tang Dynasty (7th–early 10th centuries AD) that Chang'an became the world's largest city, with a population of nearly 2 million. This was due in large part to its strategic position along the Silk Road, where the trade routes between Europe, the Middle East, and India met with China. Tea, art, silk, porcelain, religion—chiefly Islam and Buddhism—and various food goods were traded at this eastern stop along the Silk Road.

Perhaps Xi'an is best known in the West for the Terracotta Army of Emperor Qin Shi Huangdi that was unearthed in 1974. As the emperor of the Qin dynasty, Qin Shi Huangdi holds a unique—and perhaps somewhat peculiar—place in Chinese history. Often thought of in extremities, Qin Shi Huangdi

Left: *The rickshaw remains a popular mode of transportation in many Chinese cities.*

Above: *Xi'an's Terracotta Army.*

is regarded as both a megalomaniac obsessed with death (namely his own) as well as the glorious unifier and founder of the Chinese Empire. He dubbed himself the "First Emperor" of China and began the building of several defensive walls, which would later become the beginnings of the Great Wall of China. Perhaps most importantly, however, Qin Shi Huangdi is known for his thorough standardization of weights and measurements,

Above: *Lakeside pavilions, such as this one, are part of the many parks that dot the cities of China.*

for establishing a common currency consisting of round copper coins with a square center, as well as for unifying a set of laws for the entire country and standardizing Chinese writing. His legacy was indeed significant and lasting, as many of the standardizations he founded during his reign are still in use, in one form or another, today.

The Terracotta Army was commissioned by Qin Shi Huangdi in 246 BC. Over 700,000 workers were employed to build this massive, ostentatious tomb in his honor. Inside the tomb stand over 7,000 terracotta soldiers and horses, lined up in rows to protect the emperor's tomb for all eternity. Though never fully completed to Qin Shi Huangdi's specifications, the Terracotta Army still took a monumental 36 years to build. Originally painted in bright colors, the army has faded to a gray-brown hue due to the natural oxidation process. Most remarkable upon close inspection of the army, however, are the individual expressions and unique features that each warrior has been given.

Today, Xi'an is a city of over 3 million people and has one of the largest Chinese Muslim populations (referred to as the *Hui* minority) concentrated within a city center in China. There are six mosques in Xi'an alone. The most renowned of these was founded in 742 and remains one of the largest and oldest mosques in the country. In the region just outside of Xi'an's city center lies one of the Five Sacred Mountains of Daoism in China, Hua Shan, meaning "Flower Mountain." Deemed the most beautiful of the five mountains by its followers, Hua Shan is part of the Qingling Mountain Range and sits south of the Wei and Yellow Rivers. It is a pilgrimage site for ascetics, believers and others in search of the rare white fungus that grows atop this mountain and is said to offer immortality.

Today, Xi'an has one of the largest Chinese Muslim populations (referred to as the Hui *minority) concentrated within a city center in China. There are six mosques in Xi'an alone.*

Below: *Street markets containing both raw and cooked foods are an integral feature to Chinese street culture.*

In addition to the sites of Hua Shan and the Terracotta Army, Xi'an is home to several well-preserved pagodas. The most famous is the Great Wild Goose Pagoda, built in 652. It houses Buddhist scriptures brought to China from India and stands 210 feet tall. Xi'an is home to the Shaanxi History Museum and houses several tombs of emperors as well as the tomb of Empress Wu. It is one of the most important archaeological sites in China, where Neolithic villages and skeletal remains from the Paleolithic period have shaped our picture of what an early China might have looked like. Because of Xi'an's numerous and important contributions to our understanding of China's history, it remains a hub of academic and scientific inquiry as well as a major destination for visitors. Much has changed in the field of archaeology since the China of Mao's days, when relics from a dynastic, feudal China were destroyed, graves looted and historical sites destroyed. Many of these sites, such as the Terracotta Army, have become tourist attractions, serving to educate visitors on the history of one of the world's oldest civilizations.

Many of China's archaeological sites, such as the Terracotta Army, have become huge tourist attractions, serving to educate visitors on the history of one of the world's oldest civilizations.

Left: *One of China's many Daoist temples.*

Below: *The image of the setting sun over the Xi'an skyline.*

History

China is one of the longest-unified civilizations in the history of mankind. It is estimated that China has been home to humans since 8000 BC, settled by groups who congregated primarily around the Yellow, Wei, and Yangzi Rivers. The earliest skeletal remains of human ancestors unearthed in China date from sometime between 500,000 to 600,000 BC. Remains of Neanderthals and *Homo sapiens* have been discovered throughout China, proving that this country has been home to early humans for thousands of years.

Early Societies and the Role of the Emperor

The oldest and most important pottery to be discovered in China is from the Yangshao period, dating between 5000 and 3000 BC. The Yangshao culture, as it is known today, was centered in the provinces of Gansu, Shanxi, and Henan. Evidence of sophisticated agricultural practices that included the domestication of animals, the firing of pottery with kilns, growing of silk worms for the production of textiles and the use of mortar and pestles for the grinding of their staple crop of millet have been found at several sites. The most famous of these lies just outside Xi'an. Perhaps the most astounding archaeological remains found in China to date are from the Shang dynasty (1600–1050 BC). The most important of the remains uncovered from the Shang period are oracle bones, whose inscriptions display the first recorded evidence of the Chinese language. Other archaeological finds from the Shang period provide evidence that they were the first to mass-produce cast bronze.

The dynastic tradition in China has a long history and is intimately tied to the relationship between heaven and earth. Each dynasty was ruled by the emperor, who was termed the "Son of Heaven." The emperor's power to rule here on earth was said to be authorized by Heaven under the the political concept called the Mandate of Heaven. Any imbalance to his rule could be overthrown and taken away by the next ruler, who would claim that the previous emperor's right to the mandate was no longer valid because of unjust or dishonorable acts. Often, natural disasters, astronomical changes or other disruptions to earth and daily life were viewed as evidence of the decline of the dynasty and proof of wicked or evil actions taken by the emperor. Such signs, as would later be recorded by the following dynasty's historians, were proof that the Mandate of Heaven was in transition, making its cyclical change of hands to the new, noble, and magnanimous emperor.

Dynastic rule within China was thus cyclical; the legitimacy to rule always began with the removal of the Mandate of Heaven from the previous emperor, with the claim that he no longer had approval from Heaven to rule. Only then could the right to power be granted to the new dynastic ruler. Within each dynasty, however, succession was usually passed down to the firstborn son who often took the seat of the emperor as a very young child. The earliest recordings of dynastic rule in China begin with the Shang and Zhou dynasties, spanning nearly 1,400 years in total. There are six emperors associated with the earliest years of the Chinese empire, yet because of the total lack of historical evidence of the existence of these rulers, much of what we know about them remains within the realm of legend. These emperors— Fuxi, Shen Nong, Huangdi (also known as the Yellow Emperor), Yao, Shun and Yu the Great—are associated with the beginnings of hunting, fishing, and the domestication of animals, with the building of houses, writing, administration, the lunar calendar, medicine, and food cultivation. Perhaps even more than figures of power and authority, these legendary emperors are symbols of the beginnings of civilization in China.

Left: *Buddhism was one of the many imports brought to China along the Silk Road.*

Below: *Painted paper lanterns, such as this one, are popular during the Lantern Festival that follows Chinese New Year each spring.*

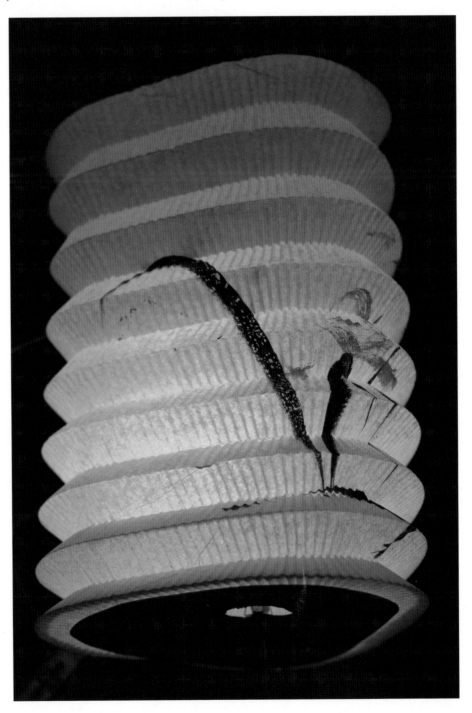

Above: *The Chinese character for "heaven," an important concept in the dynastic cycle of Chinese rule.*

Right: *The tranquil face of the Buddha.*

Qin Dynasty (221–206 BC)

The foundation of a unified Imperial China begins with Emperor Qin Shi Huangdi. The name Huangdi was borrowed from the legendary Yellow Emperor, who is said to have mythical powers and is credited with being the founder of the Chinese Empire. Although China's dynastic system began much earlier, it was Qin Shi Huangdi who would establish the dynastic cycle of emperors—a system of imperial rule that would last up until 1911, when the final Chinese dynasty would mark the end of an Imperial China. It is astounding to note that Emperor Qin Shi Huangdi set into motion a unified China through the standardization of money, measurements, legal doctrine, writing and beginning what would become the Great Wall of China in his mere 11-year reign as emperor.

Western and Eastern Han Dynasties (206 BC–220 AD)

Following the brief but pivotal Qin dynasty, which encompassed the reigns of just two emperors—Qin Shi Huangdi and his son Er Shi—a Golden Age of Chinese history began with the founding of the Han dynasty. One of the longest dynasties in Chinese history, the Han dynasty is known as the time when Confucian law began to shape the establishment of various Chinese institutions, the most famous of which is the examination system. Its first emperor, Emperor Gaodi, founded the Han dynasty in 206 BC. Gaodi quickly established the capital of his empire at Chang'an, located near modern-day Xi'an. Greatly influenced by the teachings and writings of Confucius, Gaodi set in motion a dynasty that would come to be known for its introduction of institutional and bureaucratic policy. Upon Gaodi's death, several short-lived emperors held the throne. Han Wudi, who took control of the Han dynasty in 141 BC, is best known for his huge efforts in the

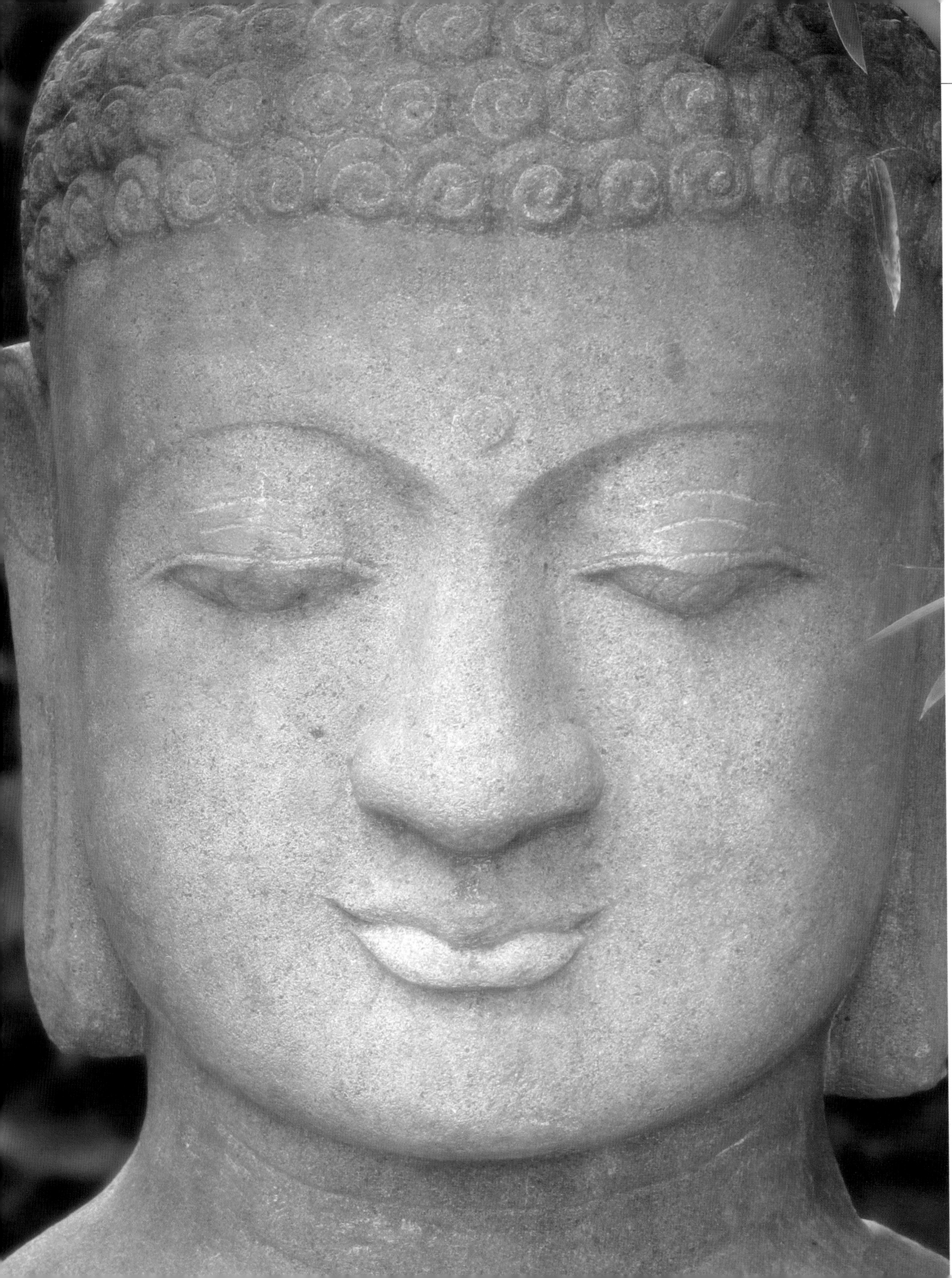

expansion of the Chinese empire. Wudi began making trips along the Silk Road, trading horses and gaining a greater understanding of the desire foreign nations had to trade with China. In addition to being known as a time of expansion and trade, the years that comprise the Han dynasty are famous for the invention of paper, the writing of the first Chinese dictionary and for the prolific spread of Buddhism.

The Han dynasty fell in 220 BC. During the subsequent 350 years, widespread warfare and instability divided China. Revived by general Yang Jian, the Sui dynasty reunified the country in 581. Like the Qin dynasty, the Sui had only two emperors but is also known as a brief but powerful time in Chinese history. Without the unification efforts of the Sui, the Tang dynasty—a second Golden Age within Chinese history—could not have taken place.

Tang Dynasty (618–907)

The Tang dynasty had a lasting impression on Chinese culture. For much of the almost 300 years of the Tang, China experienced a peace and stability it had not seen for many years. The Tang was acutely focused on expansion, amassing the largest territory China had ever seen. During the second Tang emperor's reign—Emperor Taizong—the borders of the Chinese Empire extended from Tibet into southern Siberia and from the eastern border of Korea all the way south into present-day Vietnam. It was during the Tang's control over its capital of Chang'an when the city witnessed huge growth and was renowned for being a center of culture and civilization. During this time, Chang'an experienced much diversity in the thought, religion, and cultures of its residents who, at that time, included Jews, Muslims from Persia, as well as Uighurs and Arabs from various central Asian countries.

It is estimated that China has been home to humans since 8000 BC, although the earliest human skeletal remains, unearthed in China, date from between 500,000 to 600,000 BC.

Left: *The Terracotta Army is made up of over 7,000 soldiers, each carved with an individual expression.*

Below: *The Terracotta Army was discovered by accident in 1974 by two Xi'an farmers.*

The arts of the Tang dynasty distinguish this period from many others in Chinese history. Perhaps more than any other dynasty, the Tang dynasty was *the* golden era of Chinese poetry. Widely considered to be two of the greatest Chinese poets of all time, both Li Bai (701–762) and Du Fu (712–770) lived and wrote during this prosperous period. Benefiting from the invention of paper during the Han dynasty, the Tang developed block printing, thus making written works by these poets widely available to the masses.

Painting, pottery, and silversmithing were further refined during the Tang. New styles were developed, some of which were influenced by central Asian countries, whose goods continually made their way to Chang'an via the Silk Road. Chinese goods, in turn, were transported in ever larger quantities back along the Silk Road and into India, Southeast Asia, Central Asia, and the Middle East. Buddhism continued the expansion of its sphere of influence, and both Japan and Korea began to model their cities and languages after what visitors had seen and heard during regular visits to Chang'an.

The Tang dynasty is also known for the famous Empress Wu, who was the only empress in China's history to rule in her own right. Empress Wu came to power after the death of her husband. She quickly and deftly removed her competition for the throne, including her own offspring, and ruled over the Tang for 15 years. Empress Wu found herself embroiled in controversy and scandal for much of her career as empress, partially because of her actions

Left: *Many sections of the Great Wall have been restored so that tourists may climb certain sections and explore the watchtowers.*

Right: *Built during Ming times, the wall at Badaling is one of the most popular sections of the Great Wall of China.*

immediately preceding and following her husband's death, but also because the presence of a woman in the position of ruler went against Confucian tradition at that time.

Northern and Southern Song Dynasties (960–1279)

Lasting just under 300 years, the Song dynasty is remembered for its contributions to literature and the arts, and as a time when economic development paved the way for an emerging middle class. The increased development and use of woodblock printing during the Song period enabled texts to be produced and spread to the masses, resulting in an increased interest in the writings of Confucius and higher literacy rates across the country. Calligraphy, painting, and poetry experienced a period of growth and increased appreciation. In the early thirteenth century, the Mongols invaded and captured northern China. Finally, in 1279, they overtook the Song dynasty to establish the Yuan dynasty in their northern capital of Beijing.

Yuan Dynasty (1279–1368)

As the first non-Han Chinese dynasty, the Yuan dynasty was established thanks to the efforts of their famous Mongolian leader Genghis Khan. Kublai Khan, the grandson of Genghis Khan, was sent by his grandfather to conquer China and did so in 1279 when he overthrew the Song dynasty. Kublai Khan served as the first emperor of his self-proclaimed dynasty the Yuan, meaning "Original Dynasty." Perhaps more than anything else, the Mongols are remembered for their massive empire, which extended all the way from eastern Europe to the eastern coast of China on the East China Sea. This period is also known for the subsequent communication and trade that took place between Mongolia, China, and Europe. The famous writer and traveler Marco Polo spent 21 years during this time in China under the court of Kublai Khan; much of our understanding of the interaction between Europe and China during this period can be gathered from Polo's famous writings of his time spent in China during the Yuan dynasty. A short-lived dynasty, the Yuan started to disintegrate in the mid-fourteenth century and rebellions against the Mongols broke out frequently.

Ming Dynasty (1368–1644)

The Ming dynasty took control over China following Genghis Khan's infamous rule, along with several other Mongol leaders, of northern China. Meaning "brilliant," Ming times are regarded, along with the Han and Tang dynasties, as a period of stability, unity, and peace. Establishing present-day Nanjing as his capital, Emperor Hongwu was the first Ming ruler and restored several bureaucratic policies, such as the examination system and the civil service, both of which had fallen to the wayside during Mongol rule. It was during Hongwu's reign when China's territory expanded to the southwest to include Yunnan and Guizhou; Hongwu's efforts would also pave the way for the Qing dynasty's enormous expansion even further west and north into Tibet and present-day Xinjiang province. The Ming dynasty is also known for advancements in scholarship and literature, when some of the greatest tales and texts to come out of China were written. The famous blue and white pottery was developed during Ming times. Some of these vases and other glazed objects are sold for millions of dollars at auction houses today.

Hongwu's grandson, who went on to become Emperor Yong Le, is considered the greatest of the Ming emperors. Yong Le moved his capital from Nanjing to Beijing, where he began work on the Forbidden Palace and where he initiated expansion of the Great Wall to the north and east of the new capital. During Yong Le's reign, China's presence within the foreign marketplace grew dramatically, particularly

Left: *The Forbidden City was home to several of China's most important emperors.*

Below: *Chinese Lions guard several gates throughout the Forbidden City.*

The Ming dynasty took control over China following Genghis Khan's infamous rule. Meaning "brilliant," Ming times are regarded, along with the Han and Tang dynasties, as a period of stability, unity, and peace.

Below: *The Silk Road was the technological and information highway of its day, where goods like this traditional teapot were traded.*

Right: *Pagodas are typically the central feature of Chinese temples and places of worship.*

in Southeast Asia, Japan, and the Middle East. Yong Le built an impressive fleet of ships and sent a Muslim eunuch from his court to lead expeditions as far as the east coast of Africa. It was during this period that the Portuguese first landed in Macau and began trading with China, a move that would pave the way for British traders in the years to come.

After Yong Le's rule came to an end, the Ming dynasty began its slow decline. Several of the emperors that followed Yong Le relied upon the eunuchs of their court; it was not uncommon for eunuchs, as was the case in several of China's dynasties, to use the power of the emperor to rule over the court and country. In many cases, emperors were mere puppets for a eunuch regime, as was the case throughout the latter portion of the Ming dynasty. In addition to entering a period of struggle for power, China was experiencing the first major influx of European visitors, traders, and forces within its borders. Following the leasing of Macau to Portugal in 1557, the Dutch settled a section of Taiwan, and more and more English ships began to arrive.

The Ming finally fell to the power of the Manchus, an ethnic group belonging to the region of Manchuria located in northeastern China. Yong Le had originally expanded and connected the portion of the Great Wall to the north of Beijing in order to keep the threat of Manchu invasion out of his northern territory. But, in 1644, the Manchus were allowed through the wall by mistake; they swiftly took control of Beijing and the Forbidden City, thus signaling the beginning of the Qing dynasty and the end of the Ming.

Qing Dynasty (1644-1911)

The final dynasty China would witness was the Qing, founded by the Manchus of northeastern China, later to be overthrown in 1911 by Chinese Nationalists. The Qing dynasty, meaning "pure," was a dynasty of foreign rule. As Manchu rulers gained more power, they gradually replaced many Han Chinese from their posts with Manchu officers, leading to animosity, resentment, and rivalry between the two groups. During this time, the famous "queue" hairstyle of the Manchus (a long, narrow braid worn at the back) was forced upon Han Chinese men. During Qing rule, China gained presence and authority, which would eventually lead to total control, over the regions of Tibet, Taiwan, and the northwest area of Xinjiang. Under the Qing dynasty, China experienced the greatest increase in population it had ever seen, with the total population doubling in a mere 50 years during the mid- to late eighteenth century.

The two most famous emperors of the Qing dynasty were Emperor Kangxi, the second emperor of the Qing, and his grandson, Emperor Qianlong. Emperor Kangxi held his post for an unprecedented 61 years, from 1661 to 1722, and is seen by many as China's most judicious and skillful emperor. A huge supporter of Confucianism, Kangxi made several pilgrimages to sacred mountains and sites important to the religion. He is also responsible for compiling the *Kangxi Dictionary* of 40,000 characters and for publishing the most comprehensive encyclopedia China—and indeed the world—had seen at that time. The *Kangxi Dictionary* was the most widely used dictionary of its time and became the standard dictionary of China for more than 200 years. In addition to these scholarly efforts, Kangxi is known for expanding China's territorial and economic powers and for protecting the rural peasantry.

Kangxi's grandson, Emperor Qianlong, took the throne several years after Kangxi's mysterious death in 1722. Qianlong is perhaps best known for being the emperor who expanded China to its largest extent of

more than 4 million square miles. Shortly after Qianlong's exit as emperor in 1795 (he deliberately resigned after 60 years of rule so as not to surpass his grandfather's record), the Qing dynasty started to become weakened by a series of foreign powers, wars with European countries, and internal chaos. The nineteenth century was, as many scholars of China agree, one of the most chaotic, unstable, tempestuous times in the whole of Chinese history. The two Opium Wars—the first erupting in 1839, the second in 1856—fought against Britain humiliated and devastated China, resulting in mass opium dependency and causing embarrassment and loss of face to the Qing court. The loss of the first Opium War to the British led to the signing of the Treaty of Nanjing in 1842, which opened five crucial ports to the West for trade. The Treaty of Nanjing also handed Hong Kong over to British rule and began China's involvement—both forced and voluntary—with Europe and, eventually, the United States.

The fourteen-year Taiping Rebellion was another factor in the downfall of the Qing dynasty and, moreover, of Imperial China. Between 1850 and 1851, a southern peasant by the name of Hong Xiuquan amassed an estimated 30,000 followers in a scant three years. Believing him to be the younger Chinese brother of Jesus Christ, Hong Xiuquan was converted to Christianity by missionaries in his hometown of Guangzhou and led tens of thousands of Chinese peasants to the northern city of Nanjing, where they captured the city. By the time Hong Xiuquan and his followers from the south reached Nanjing, he had gathered more than one million followers and captured 600 Chinese cities. After years of fighting and bloodshed, during which an estimated 20 million people died, the Qing, who were assisted by American and English forces, recaptured Nanjing from the Taiping.

Below: *Emperor Qin Shi Huangdi was responsible for standardizing the money of China. Coins such as these became the currency during Qin times.*

Right: *The Black Dragon Pool in the ancient city of Lijiang in Yunnan province.*

Following the Taiping Rebellion, the Qing dynasty experienced a brief period of peace. It was not long, however, before the dynasty fell once again to instability and disruption. The infamous and scandalous Empress Dowager Cixi was an imperial concubine who took power of the Qing dynasty through her son, Emperor Tongzhi, when he took the throne at an impressionable 5 years of age. She ruled China, using various young emperors as her puppets, until her death in 1908. China's defeat by Japan in the Sino-Japanese War of 1894-95 brought an even greater foreign presence to China. Various other nations capitalized on the weak position of this now immense and potentially powerful country. Germany gained a presence in Shandong province and Japan moved into Russia and Korea, further threatening China.

Left: *The massive Marble Boat at Kunming Lake in the Summer Palace is made of wood and painted white to give the illusion of marble.*

Below: *One of the many canals within the Forbidden City.*

During the final years of the nineteenth century and the first years of the twentieth, several of China's internal forces and factions saw the need for reform and modernization. During this period, a scholar of medicine and native of the southern province of Guangdong, Sun Yat-Sen was amassing foreign support in both America and Britain for the establishment of a Chinese republic. Sun Yat-Sen founded the Revolutionary Alliance, intended to overthrow the Qing dynasty with the hope of establishing a republic and uniting the 15 provinces that comprised China at that time. Sen dreamed of a more democratic China, where voting, legislative, and administrative powers would be established and enacted by the people. After a series of uprisings throughout the country, Sun Yat-Sen was inaugurated on January 1, 1912 as the first president of the Chinese Republic.

Early Days of the Republic

Sun Yat-Sen's stint as president of the newfound republic was short-lived. Shortly after his inauguration, he was forced to flee the country and soon thereafter, in 1916, he died. Following Sen's establishment of the republic, two political parties emerged and began to gain support within China: the Nationalist Party—also known as the Kuomintang, the party under which Sen began his presidency—and the Communist Party. General Chiang Kai-Shek assumed power in 1926, after Sun Yat-Sen's forced removal and subsequent death. Initially, the Communist Party and the Nationalists came together in an effort to unite the country and further establish the republic that Sen had worked so hard to found. But, in 1926, Nationalists forced Communists out of the party and Chiang Kai-Shek himself ordered the killing of several Communists in Shanghai. The Communists fled from Shanghai and Nanjing, where they were headquartered, to the countryside where they remained until the Long March of 1934. Capitalizing on the weaknesses resulting from internal struggles for

Below: *The long single braid typical of the queue hairstyle that was enforced by the Manchus during the Qing dynasty.*

Right: *Ornamental archways like this one are typical features to parks, buildings, and tombs.*

power, the Japanese invaded China in 1931 and occupied Nanjing, among other northern cities. The Japanese invasion of Nanjing was so violent and horrific that it is often referred to as "The Rape of Nanjing."

Between 1926 and 1934, the Communists, led by Mao Zedong, a young leader from Hunan province known for his skill as a military strategist, fought the Kuomintang throughout the countryside with his newly formed Red Army. In 1934, pushed into the countryside and with food and medical supplies waning, Mao made the executive decision to leave the southeastern province of Jiangxi for the northeast along with 100,000 Communists. This trek, now known as the Long March, took roughly one year and was a harrowing journey

Left: *The Beijing Opera was just one of many traditional arts to be banned during the Cultural Revolution.*

Below: *Opera masks like these are worn by the jing, or "painted faces," characters of the Beijing Opera.*

through several mountain ranges and over numerous rivers. Fighting the Kuomintang most of the way, the Communists walked just under 6,000 miles through 12 provinces, and lost several thousand troops along the way. On October 19, 1935, Mao and his army arrived in the city of Yan'an, declaring it an independent Communist state.

Communist Rule and The People's Republic of China

By 1945, the Japanese had withdrawn from China and civil unrest began erupting across the country. In 1949, Chiang Kai-Shek fled China for Taiwan, where he set up a Nationalist government and remained until his death in 1975. On October 1, 1949, Mao Zedong announced the founding of the People's Republic of China (PRC) from the steps of Beijing's Tian'an Men Square.

Below: *Mao worked to simplify Chinese characters in an effort to educate the rural masses.*

Right: *Traditional lanterns overlook Victoria Harbor in Hong Kong during Chinese New Year.*

Mao, in an effort to unite the country, began a series of land reforms in the early 1950s. Viewing cities as evidence of the encroachment of Western bourgeois ideology and lifestyle, Mao looked to the peasants of the countryside to forge China's new future as a Communist nation. Mao began to redistribute land and relocate households. Between 1955 and 1956, he arranged for cooperative farms to be set up all across rural China. By the late 1950s, private ownership of land had been abolished and the *danwei* (work unit) system was put into place. From that time forward, each citizen of the new People's Republic of China belonged to a danwei, which tied him or her to the hierarchy of the Communist Party. The *danwei* in China serves simultaneously as a sort of community, family, and micro-society; through the hierarchies of the *danwei*, one receives permission for travel, relocation and other changes in employment, marriage, and even having children. Food and other daily matters are also channeled through one's *danwei*. Without a *danwei*, even today, daily life becomes nearly impossible.

In 1958, Mao launched the Great Leap Forward in an effort to develop the countryside and promote productivity. By this time, there were already nearly 23,500 communes across the countryside. Many deemed as intellectuals, too Western or bourgeois were sent to various locations in rural China to be "re-educated." Mao urged the new landless proletariat to reach unrealistic productivity goals; the tasks for production were assigned down to the workers by the Party cadres, who then redistributed the goods back up the chain of authority, and eventually to the state. This resulted in the unequal distribution of grain, which in turn led to mass starvation. Widespread famines affected China between 1959 and 1961, during which time an estimated 30 million people died of starvation throughout the country.

Mao's next target—culture—would lead to the Cultural Revolution, a campaign to reform the feudal, imperialist remnants of the old China. In 1965, Mao launched the Cultural Revolution and instructed thousands of China's youth to take to the villages, streets, and cities to weed out any remnants of the "four olds": old culture, old customs, old ideologies, and old habits. Religion was outlawed during this time, along with old customs, traditions, and art forms, such as Chinese opera. Mao held several rallies during the years of the Cultural Revolution at Tian'an Men Square, where his Red Guards would gather in their thousands to receive instructions from their Great (*weida*) Leader. The Red Guards—mainly students in their 20s—traveled the country destroying temples and burning books, clothing, musical instruments, and artwork. They demoralized, publicly criticized, and abused teachers and intellectuals, even killing anyone thought to be connected with the West. Public denunciation and embarrassment of men and women, who formerly had been treated with much respect, resulted in widespread suicide. Universities in China closed during this period, many of which did not reopen until the late 1970s. Rural "Cadre Schools" were set up in 1968, where some 130,000 people were sent for "reeducation," involving manual labor and schooling to undo "capitalist" ideologies and tendencies.

Much debate surrounds discussion of the Cultural Revolution. Many suspect that the Cultural Revolution was, at its core, Mao's response to increasing dissent within the Party. It is also interpreted as an effort made by Mao to reinvigorate the Communist Party with the revolutionary spirit of China's youth. Some of the most horrific acts of the Cultural Revolution have been attributed to the "Gang of Four," who included Mao's wife. They

Left: *Mao statues fill the squares of China, reminding all of his legacy to this country's history.*

Above: *During the Cultural Revolution, Mao reached near-godlike status. Even today, images of him fill curio shops aimed at tourists.*

The years between 1968 and Mao's death in 1976 were filled with turmoil and massive discord between Mao and other high-ranking members of the Chinese Communist Party.

were arrested in 1976, over ten years after the beginning of the Cultural Revolution, and became the political scapegoats for nearly everything that had gone wrong during the decade between 1966 and 1976.

Within the Communist Party, the years between 1968 and Mao's death in 1976 were filled with turmoil and massive discord between Mao and other high-ranking members of the Chinese Communist Party (CCP). Successors to Mao, including Liu Shaoqi and Lin Biao, were denounced and arrested, accused of conspiring to overthrow Mao. The Gang of Four were formally arrested shortly after Mao's death in September 1976. Their trial in the autumn of 1980 was watched on television by millions of Chinese citizens.

Following Mao's death, the CCP appointed Deng Xiaoping as the leader of the People's Republic. Deng's leadership is primarily remembered through his massive economic reforms and the subsequent opening up of China to the West, particularly to the United States. While economic freedom may have been promoted and experienced through Deng Xioping's reforms, civil freedoms still went largely ignored by the Chinese government. During the mid-1980s, many pro-democracy rallies were held by students in nearly two dozen Chinese cities, calling for freedom of speech, freedom of assembly, and free elections. These demonstrations culminated at Tian'an Men Square in the summer of 1989, where over 100,000 students occupied the square. For six weeks, students occupied the square, leading hunger strikes and peacefully protesting the civil rights abuses of their country. On June 4, 1989 troops opened fire on the students in Tian'an Men as well as students protesting in both Shanghai and Chengdu, the capital

Right and Below: *Mao's face on the one-yuan note: a sign of the significance of this leader to the history of China.*

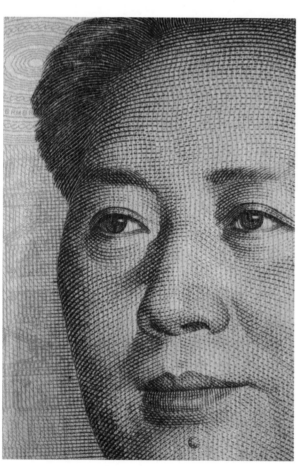

中国人民银行

1

壹圆

116

of Sichuan province. It is estimated that thousands of student protestors were killed and many more were wounded and imprisoned; however, the exact number of casualties is unknown because of the government's refusal to release the names of those massacred. China suffered international criticism and economic sanctions from countries all over the world in response to the horrific actions taken by Chinese officials in response to the students' nonviolent protest. To this day, the Chinese government refuses to publicly acknowledge the massacre that took place in 1989.

During the end of the twentieth century and in the first years of the twenty-first, China crossed several landmarks toward positioning itself as a major economic and technological presence in the world. In 2001, China was admitted to the World Trade Organization and in 2003 the first Chinese astronaut, Yang Liwei, went into space. China is currently preparing for its role as host to both the 2008 Summer Olympics in Beijing and the 2010 World Expo, to be held in Shanghai. Despite many major advancements, much of the country's population suffers from an ever-widening gap between the rich and the poor, from rigid bureaucracy and from insufficient medical care and facilities.

Spanning nearly 10,000 years from its beginnings during the Neolithic period, China's history tells of many impressive feats of human endeavor. Home to one of the world's oldest continuous civilizations, China's culture is an enduring enterprise. Considering that much of what constitutes Chinese culture—language, religion, societal beliefs—has been in place for thousands of years, it is unlikely that Chinese culture could be swept away overnight with the growth of globalization.

In 2001, China was admitted to the World Trade Organization and in 2003 the first Chinese astronaut, Yang Liwei, went into space.

Left: *To many, Hong Kong symbolizes China's modern future.*

Below: *The flag of the People's Republic of China.*

Beijing

The Forbidden City, built during the Ming dynasty in the 15th century, was home to various emperors of China until the Qing dynasty, the final dynasty in China's history.

Since the days of Kublai Khan and the Mongol Yuan dynasty, Beijing—meaning "northern capital," once called Peking—has been the capital of China. Best known for its historic sites such as Tian'an Men Square, the Forbidden City and Summer Palace, Beijing is also a modern center of scholarly achievement, a bastion of contemporary art, with a vibrant music and club scene and plenty of shopping hub to boot. Though Beijing lies within Hebei province, it forms its own autonomous administrative municipality. The climate of Beijing is extreme, experiencing intensely humid and hot summers and cold, dry winters. Home to a growing population of over 9 million, Beijing embodies aspects of both old and new China.

The area we know today to be Beijing and the surrounding province of Hebei were, according to archaeological records, home to some of the oldest ancestors of humans. Just outside Beijing, archaeologists found the remnants of over 40 bodies dating to about 700,000 years old in 1927. One of these bodies was given the name "Peking Man." The remains are among some of the oldest fossils of hominids to ever be unearthed. Archaeologists believe Peking Man and the 39 other bipedal skeletons found are the ancient ancestors of modern-day Chinese people.

Still in the center of this massive, energetic capital sits the Forbidden City. Built during the Ming dynasty in the 15th century, this grand palace was home to various emperors of China until the Qing dynasty, the final dynasty in China's history. Halls, courts, offices and residences make up the bulk of the Forbidden City, making it the largest network of ancient buildings within China. In ancient times, commoners were not allowed inside the gates of the Forbidden City; only the emperor and his entourage— including eunuchs, concubines, consorts and other appointees—lived inside the walls of the palace, giving it the name "forbidden."

In ancient times, commoners were not allowed inside the gates of the Forbidden City.

Known for its symmetry and placement of buildings along a north-south axis, the Forbidden City is a prime example of the principles of *feng shui*.

Lying just outside the walls of this historic fortress are where the remnants of the old neighborhoods can be found. These neighborhoods, called *hutong* in Chinese, consist of a series of tiny, crowded alleyways that surround courtyard houses once occupied by officials to the court. Today, there are around 4,000 *hutong* in Beijing, but they are quickly diminishing, as the city has already seen the destruction of 2,000 *hutong* within the past 50 years. It is within these traditional *hutong* where one can truly glimpse what life for a Beijing resident might have been like 200-300 years ago. Tours of traditional hutong are possible today, where a guide can take tourists by foot

Left: *Vegetable vendors line the back streets of all major Chinese cities.*

Below: *Traffic clogs one of Beijing's many ring roads.*

Covering over 800 acres of land, the "Garden of Good Health and Harmony" is an example of excellent feng shui, *the Chinese system of geomancy which, when used correctly, is said to offer wealth, health and harmony to places and their inhabitants.*

Below: *Revolutionary statues sit in front of the Mausoleum that holds the embalmed body of Mao at Tian'an Men Square*

or pedicab through these quaint, winding alleys. There, children play under the close watch of their grandparents, who often sit on small wooden stools, chatting with neighbors, playing card games, or drinking a cup of tea.

The most famous of all the Beijing *hutong* sits in the area north of the Forbidden City and Bei Hai Park. This park, with its large white Tibetan-style pagoda, overlooks the tranquil Bei Hai Lake. Originally an imperial garden, Bei Hai Park is filled with paddleboats during summer months when families come out to enjoy the sunshine and warm weather. At the northern tip of Bei Hai Lake is the famous Gulou *hutong*, where lotus flower vendors, fruit and vegetable stalls, and various men in pedicabs looking for their next customer can all be found.

The 2001 film *Beijing Bicycle* takes place within one of the many Beijing *hutong*. It depicts the life of a young boy living in Beijing during a time of transition and turmoil. In addition to the portrayal of life inside a Beijing *hutong*, *Beijing Bicycle* comments on the significance of the bicycle, not merely as a mode of transport for most Beijingers, but as a symbol for China itself. Anyone who visits this crowded capital will marvel at the throngs of bicyclists that fill up the major roads each morning and afternoon. First introduced to China by American tourists in 1891, it is estimated that the bicycle is ridden today by 370 million Chinese and by 7 million Beijing residents alone. China is the world's leading bicycle manufacturer, producing nearly 41 million bicycles each year.

During the summer months when the Beijing heat was too stifling for the royal court, the Summer Palace served as an airy

Above: *A setting sun over Kunming Lake at the Summer Palace.*

getaway. Set among 3 lakes, shaded hills and several walkways, the Summer Palace exists largely due to the Empress Dowager Cixi, who built the palace in 1888 to commemorate her 60th birthday. In 1900, the Summer Palace was destroyed during the Boxer uprising but was quickly rebuilt 3 years later by Cixi. Covering over 800 acres of land, the "Garden of Good Health and Harmony" is an example of excellent *feng shui*, the Chinese system of geomancy which, when used correctly, is said to offer wealth, health and harmony to places and, accordingly, the people who use them.

On the outskirts of Beijing are the tombs of 13 Ming emperors, stretching out over 15 square miles. The Ming Tombs are considered the finest example of imperial tomb architecture and of *feng shui* burial alignment. Upon approaching the tombs, the 4-mile causeway is lined with various statues of animals, soldiers and officials. During its long construction, each Ming emperor had a say in the location and aesthetic features of his tomb. The first emperor to be buried at this auspicious site was Yong Le, along with his wife and 16 of his concubines. Excavations of the Ming tombs have uncovered numerous artifacts and treasures from the Ming era.

Just beyond the Ming Tombs, the easternmost reaches of the Great Wall of China can be seen sprawling along the mountainous landscape just outside the capital. A large portion of the wall that sits outside Beijing, originally built during the Ming dynasty, has since been restored for the benefit of tourists and historic purposes. Not a priority to every dynasty in China, the construction of the Great Wall began with the earliest dynastic rule in China, the Qin, and was completed during the second-to-last dynasty—the Ming. In each section of the wall, local materials were used in its construction. During the early building of the wall, in the Qin dynasty, a rammed-earth technique was used. Later, the Ming used a combination of brick and stone. The wall is made up of a series of towers, signal beacons, ramparts and treacherous walkways, all designed with the specific purpose of discouraging enemies from penetrating into China. Built at least two arrow shots between each other, the towers served as living quarters for the watchmen who guarded them. The walkways between each tower each contain irregular steps, designed to make the climbing of the wall more difficult for intruders attempting to overtake the tower guards. The portions of the Great Wall that lie just outside Beijing are the best preserved portions of the wall, although other sections can be found in Qinghai, Gansu and Shanxi provinces.

Since the establishment of the People's Republic of China (PRC) in 1949, Beijing has reopened many of its historic sites and has seen more tourists bound through its gates than ever before. As the center of a China that Mao envisaged, Beijing was the first to feel the dramatic changes that the introduction of communism to China, including such historical events of this period as the Cultural Revolution, brought about. As the seat of Chairman Mao's Republic, Beijing was where thousands of Red Guards congregated and held meetings. Tian'an Men Square has traditionally been the center of such large-scale meetings and demonstrations, from Mao's declaration on October 1, 1949 of the founding of the PRC, to his frequent speeches to the Red Guard in the early days of the Cultural Revolution, to the catastrophic 1989 student protests. Surrounding this giant square sit

Beijing's buildings, streets and squares tell the story of the great changes that this capital has witnessed over the years. Still growing, the look and feel of Beijing continues to transform before our very eyes.

Left: *The lion is the guardian figure of many temples and palaces in China.*

Below: *Trees fill the landscape of Chinese parks and gardens.*

numerous tourist and government buildings, including the Great Hall of the People, Mao's Mausoleum, China National Museum and the Qian Men Tower. Mao's Mausoleum is open to the public: there, his embalmed body is still on display most mornings and afternoons. Beijing's buildings, streets and squares tell the story of the great changes that this capital has witnessed over the years.

Today, as Beijing gears up for its role as host to the 2008 Summer Olympics, the city continues with its inexorable plan of modernization. Massive cranes and construction projects fill Beijing's skyline, and the city has promised a thorough rejuvenation of the capital to include more green space and lawns. Confronted with debilitating traffic and dangerous air pollution caused by increasing number of cars within the city limits, the Chinese government placed a ban on outward expansion of its capital in 2005. Still growing within its city limits, however, the look and feel of Beijing continues to transform before our very eyes.

Left: *Vendors selling Chinese goods.*

Above: *Mao's picture still faces the crowds that gather at Tian'an Men Square.*

Food reigns supreme in all aspects of Chinese culture. Historically the Chinese have linked food to social, familial, and even political institutions through the household stove and practices like banqueting.

Below: *Mooncakes are just one example of the festival food of China.*

Right: *Tea is China's most consumed beverage.*

Food

Nearly everything involving food in China—from the kitchen and the Kitchen God, to banqueting and toasting, to the traditional concepts of *yin* and *yang* that incorporate different dishes into a philosophy of eating where balance is tantamount—are part and parcel of what it means to be Chinese. Rice, the center of any Chinese meal, has been a staple crop in the south since 10,000 BC. When soy was introduced in the north, tofu and soy sauce entered the Chinese diet to become central ingredients in any meal. While the north historically focused on millet as its primary grain crop, rice has been part of the Chinese diet for thousands of years. Rice is so central to any meal that asking if one has eaten is, taken literally, asking if they have eaten rice. However, it is important to note, that no meal is complete if it does not include accompanying side dishes (called *cai*) to be consumed with the rice. These dishes, usually cooked, typically include various vegetable and meat dishes. *Cai*, then, is what defines a cuisine as regional, as each province has its own special versions of *cai*.

From the Shandong cuisine of the Northeast to Shanghai cuisine of central China, and from the fiery dishes of Sichuan down to the subtle and understated flavors of Cantonese cuisine, each region of China has its own distinct flavor. Shandong cuisine, which is what the food of Beijing is largely based on, is considered the oldest of all the cuisines of China. Here is where you find Beijing Duck or Mongolian Hotpot as well as tangy and sour dishes like Sweet and Sour Fish or Mu Shu Pork. In addition to being thought of as the origin of Chinese cuisine, the region surrounding Shandong is rife with fertile ground perfect for cultivating crops such as barley, peanuts, soy, millet, wheat, and sorghum. Fed and nourished by the Yellow River, the food of Shandong has become synonymous with Chinese food in general.

The food of central China, including Shanghai, Huaiyang, and Suzhe cuisines, tends to focus around rice and fish. Surrounded by lakes, rivers and the Yellow Sea to the east, this region prides itself on its maritime dishes. Fermented bean curd is also a specialty of this region, alongside dishes with freshwater crabmeat, pork belly, and lotus root. Various exotic mushrooms are also native to this region, as well as the popular Keemun red tea that grows in southern Anhui province. Southwestern Chinese cuisine, by comparison, is filled with chilies, peppers and the Sichuan peppercorn called *hua jiao* that has no equivalent in any spice in the western world. Common dishes include spicy eggplant, soft tofu in a peppery red sauce, and Kung Pao Chicken. The people of Sichuan are especially proud of their gastronomical history and will gladly offer any visitor a sample of the regional delicacies.

Commonly known as Cantonese food, southern Chinese cuisine belongs to the provinces of Guangdong and Fujian, including Hong Kong, Macau, and the island of Hainan. Cantonese food is perhaps best known through *dim sum*, an assortment of small dishes that is typically eaten anytime between mid-morning to mid-afternoon, not dissimilar to a Western notion of brunch. Never eaten at dinnertime, *dim sum*—meaning "snack" in Cantonese— is usually accompanied with tea and includes such dishes as suckling pig, chicken feet, pork dumplings or spareribs. Many visitors to the province of Guangdong, particularly its capital of Guangzhou, can't help but notice the importance the southern Chinese place on food and eating. The animal and vegetable markets of this bustling city are packed with people and animals—dead and living—and is a social event in itself, where vendors and buyers argue and discuss prices, where children run around playing in the packed alleyways and where elderly men and women gamble with cards or mahjong.

Left: *Seafood is an important staple of the Chinese diet, particularly in coastal, river, and lake regions.*

Below: *Rice is the center of any meal in China. Many products, such as noodles, flour, and wines, are made from this extremely important grain.*

Markets are often centers of social activity within a city; they are the spaces where heated debates may erupt or where neighbors greet and chat over the rising prices of fish or tea. If the market serves as a locus for community life, the kitchen serves as the nucleus of family life. The kitchen in China is the center of the household; it is the space where the family gathers and where the most concern and energy is devoted to when building a home. In traditional China, a household is defined through the stove and, thus, through the kitchen, food, and eating. Those who share a stove are considered family and, likewise, those who are considered to be family are considered so precisely because they share the household stove. The dividing of the stove (which is equated with dividing the household, usually between a son and his wife and children from his parents, other siblings and perhaps other extended family members) is a powerful symbol of family unity and membership. Indeed, it is the symbol of the family in China. Hence, food is the center of home life in China and is that which binds family members to each household.

If the stove is the center of the household in China (or at least once was), then banqueting is the center of nearly every business deal, negotiation or gaining what in China is referred to as *guanxi*. A notoriously difficult word to translate, the most common translations for *guanxi* include "connections" or "relationships." More broadly, however, *guanxi* loosely refers to a social network that is employed by nearly every individual within China. While one may use *guanxi* to gain a good price on train tickets, it also may be used politically at all levels of the government hierarchy. In such transactions, it is not unlikely and in fact could be said that it would be highly irregular, for a banquet—big or small—to take place to reinforce and secure the relations established through guanxi. The importance of the banquet within the working world in China cannot be underestimated. Indeed, a banquet is the social interaction that lubricates what might otherwise be an awkward business meeting. During such banquets, food becomes secondary to the necessary toasts that are merely a small aspect to the world of *guanxi*. Comradeship (*ganqing* in Mandarin) is strengthened through the social interactions made possible in banquets.

Drinking tea in China is a major pastime. Still the most popular drink of the land, tea is as ubiquitous as water. The most common type of tea is green tea and is typically preferred during the warm months in China, whereas "red tea," or black tea, is considered a cold-weather drink because of its warming properties. Milk, sugar, or lemon is never added to tea in China, and any additive that a certain type of tea may have (jasmine or chrysanthemum flowers being the most common) takes place during the fermentation process. Oolong tea—the most fermented of the teas—is the most prized tea of China, especially Fujianese oolong called *tie guanyin*. It is named after the Buddhist goddess of mercy and compassion *Guan Yin*. For over 5,000 years, China has made an art of growing, processing, fermenting, drinking and even trading this ancient beverage.

Various alcoholic beverages are also popular in China. First introduced by Europeans in the early 20th century, beer is found everywhere in China. Tsingtao and Yanjing are the most widely consumed brands. Wine can be found in China, albeit in small quantities as most Chinese prefer grain-based alcoholic drinks to grape-based spirits. Grain wine, referred to as *baijiu* meaning "white spirits" in Chinese, is the most popular drink for toasting at banquets. *"Gan bei!"* (Bottoms up! or, literally, "dry the cup") is the toast you'll hear when raising a

Left: *Dried goods, including fish, are used in culinary dishes all over the country, particularly in the food of central China.*

Above: *Chinese goods like these can be found in various Chinatowns all over the world.*

cup of this exceedingly strong liquor whose alcoholic content can reach anywhere between 80 and 120 proof (40-60% pure alcohol). One popular variety of *baijiu* is called *erguotou*, a clear yet potent beverage distilled from sorghum and drunk by Beijing workers.

The introduction of fast food to China has, some would argue, changed the consumption practices of its people. Fast food has also contributed to the relationship its citizens have with food and the social spaces of eating. While some, both inside and outside China, condemn the increasing effect globalization has had on ancient culinary practices and beliefs, others have illustrated how the introduction of more and more Western products into China has a far more complicated effect on the Chinese population than first assumed. For example, the sight of a woman eating alone in public is often received with suspicion. Because eating in China is such a communal event, eating alone, particularly a woman eating alone, is considered not only out of the ordinary but a deviant act. In contrast to the domestic space of the kitchen, the public space of the restaurant has traditionally in China been a threatening space for women. With the introduction of fast-food chain eateries, like McDonalds or Pizza Hut or even Starbucks, a woman eating alone in such an environment is not considered unusual or threatening in the way it might be in a more traditional Chinese-style restaurant. Such examples of the ways in which eating and the spaces in which one eats further demonstrate how China continues to adapt to its place within a global food market.

In China, food signifies much more than just a meal; it is both a way of life and living as well as a means of securing one's place and status as a social being. Perhaps more so in China than anywhere else does the aphorism "you are what you eat" ring true.

Below: *It is considered very bad manners to place a pair of chopsticks upright in a bowl of rice, because it resembles offerings made to the dead.*

Above: *Southern Chinese cuisine is home to some of the most diverse ingredients—like these cockle and grasshopper kebabs!*

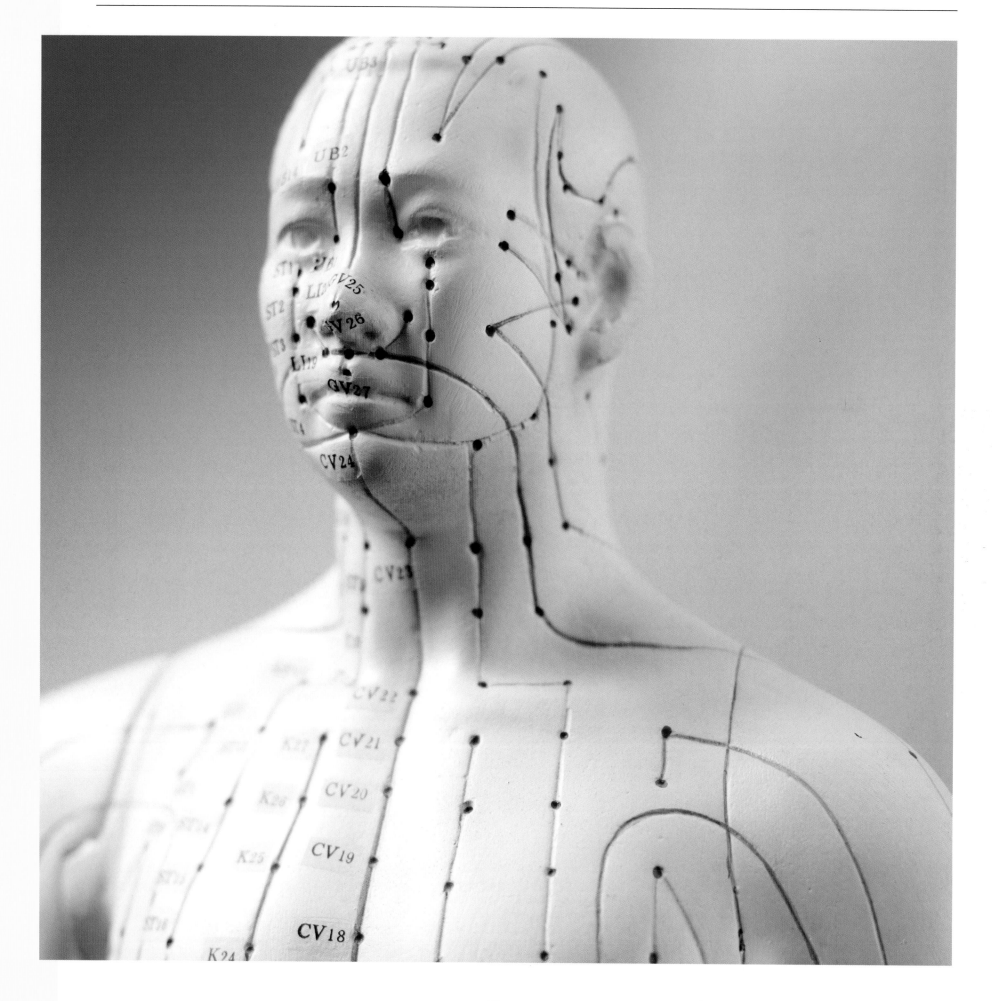

Medicine

Traditional Chinese Medicine (TCM), as it is referred to today, refers to the medical practices of China that have developed over the past 4,000 years. Medicine within China has a long history and involves the body as it interacts with its surrounding environment and the universe. It is therefore no coincidence that the earliest records of the written Chinese language were also medical records, written on oracle bones during the Shang dynasty (1750–1040 BC). The teachings, practices, and philosophy of Traditional Chinese Medicine began with the legendary Yellow Emperor. Chinese medicine bases many of its tenets on his exhaustive volume *The Yellow Emperor's Classic of Medicine*. This text became particularly popular within Daoism, particularly because of its concentration on immortality, which attracted the interest of many Daoist scholars as well as the famous emperor Qin Shi Huangdi. The text also lays out the foundations for what would become the medical practices of China we are familiar with today, discussing the theories of *qi*, and of *yin* and *yang*. The Yellow Emperor's Classic of Medicine discusses food as related to health, as well as the practices of diagnosis and treatment.

Centered on concepts such as *qi* and *yin* and yang, Traditional Chinese Medicine is often thought of as a holistic medical practice. Traditional medicine within China views the body as a gift that one receives from one's parents, and therefore it should not be mutilated in any way. The body is a site for energy and balance, working with the external world constantly to remain balanced and whole. At the root of this energy is *qi*. *Qi* is what gives life to everything in the universe and produces the opposing yet cyclical forces of *yin* and *yang*. Nearly every aspect of life is affected by *qi*; in addition to being the

Centered on concepts such as qi *and* yin *and* yang, *Traditional Chinese Medicine is often thought of as a holistic medical practice.*

Left: *This mannequin displays the meridians and pressure points that the flow of qi moves along within the body.*

Below: *Ginseng, tea, and acupuncture needles are a common sight in any TCM practitioner's office.*

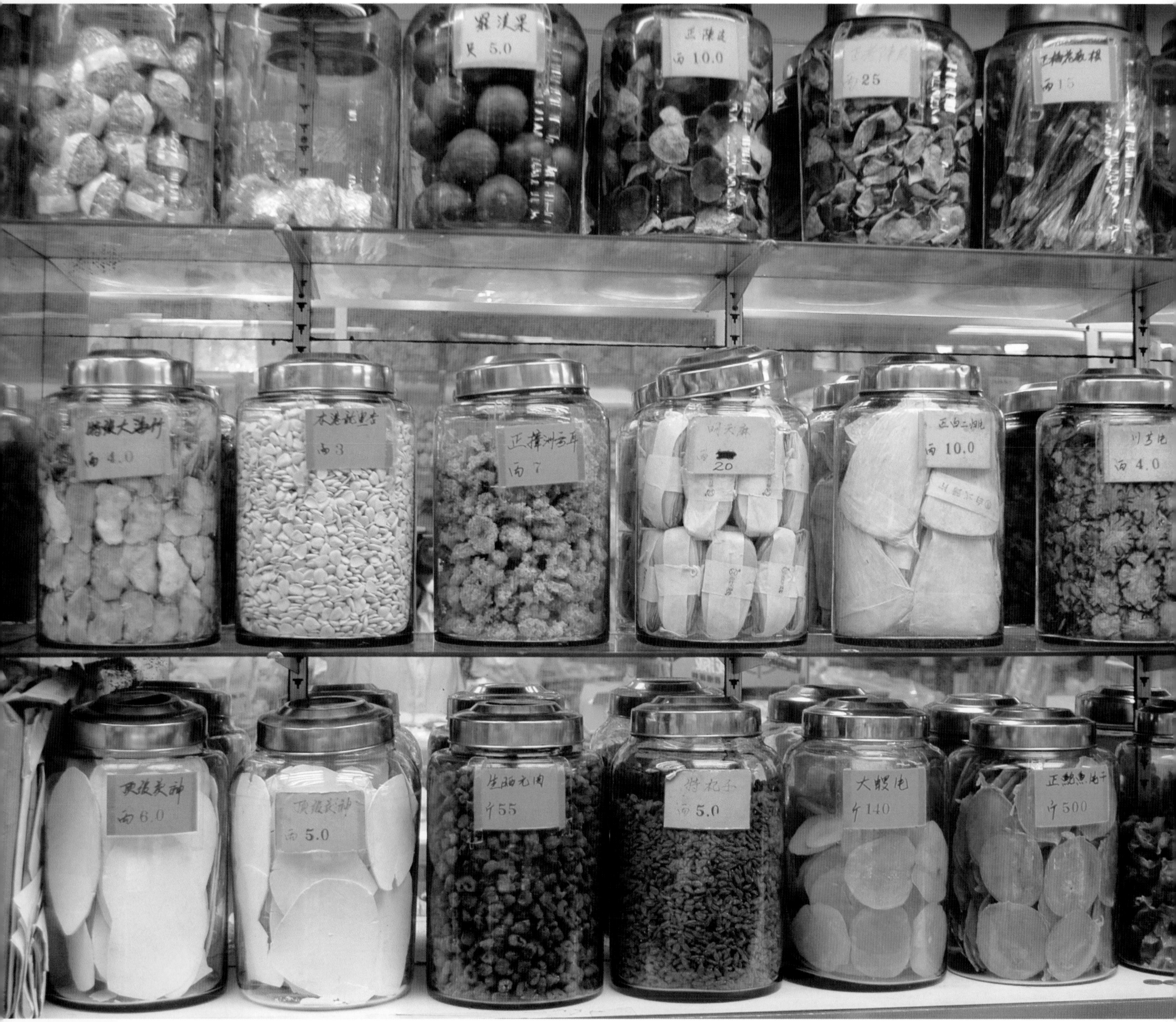

key concept behind TCM, *qi* also shapes art, architecture, religion and bodily practices such as *qigong* and *taijiquan*.

Within the human body, *qi* flows through a network of meridians, or channels, that move through every part of the body. The center of *qi* within the human body lies just below the navel, and from there 12 meridians radiate out through the body, traveling through all of the vital organs. Acupuncture and acupressure are based on these meridians, utilizing specific points on various parts of the body to either hasten or slow the movement of *qi* through the body. The act of applying pressure or inserting needles at these points is an attempt to balance the forces of *yin* and *yang* within the body, thus gaining greater balance and well-being. Unlike Western medicine, which views viruses and bacteria as the causes of illness in the body, TCM looks to inner imbalance as the root of all illness and malady. In this way, Chinese medicine views illness as rising from within the body, and less upon external, communicable causes of sickness.

If *qi* is the flow of energies in the body, *yin* and *yang* are the elements that affect this flow and create greater harmony or minor imbalances throughout one's life. While both *yin* and *yang* are opposites, they are energies that complement and rely upon each other, constantly in motion and flux. Not only does every living being correlate to having either a *yin* or *yang* energy, everything is an amalgamation of both energies, thus relying upon each to maintain harmony within the universe. *Yin* is associated with the night, darkness, the moon and women, whereas *yang* is associated with day, lightness, the sun and men. Transformation and interdependence between these two elements is integral to the understanding of *yin* and *yang*. Within food, *yin* and *yang* play an important role to not

The concept of qi has shaped nearly every aspect of Chinese life including, art, architecture, religion and bodily practices such as qigong *and* taijiquan.

Left: *A Traditional Chinese Medicine shop in Hong Kong.*

Below: *Various insects are used in medicines and remedies within TCM.*

only what is considered to be a good meal according to taste but according to health as well. Foods that have a cooling effect are considered *yin* foods, such as vegetables or tofu. These complement their *yang* counterparts: dishes that are usually heated and spiced, typically found in most meat dishes. Chinese food always seeks to gain balance, thus the elements of *yin* and *yang* guide the dietetics of China.

Nearly all of the medicines used within TCM are extracted from plants, animals, or even minerals. There are over 8,000 different kinds of herbal medicines and remedies pharmacists within China prescribe. These include treatments for anything from sexual impotence to dry skin to poor kidney function or even dysentery. Tea is perhaps the most common and most drinkable medicine in China. Different types of tea provide either cooling or heating properties, and can assist with problems of aging, for example. The Chinese people have been drinking tea for medicinal purposes since the Han dynasty.

The legend of the discovery of tea is also the story of how tea came to be used as a medicinal, restorative drink. The mythical emperor Shen Nong, as the tale goes, instructed people to boil their water before drinking it. Convinced of the health benefits of doing so, Shen Nong was sitting under a tree one day with his boiled water when a leaf from the tree above him fell into his cup. Surprised at the combined good taste and seemingly restorative properties, Shen Nong went on to try other variations of "tea" to test their health benefits. Some of these, it is claimed, were poisonous and found to be useful as an antidote. Even today, many Chinese remedies for illness come in the form of a tea. Herbs are ground up, mixed and boiled to make a specific remedy.

Below: *China has helped to highlight the medicinal properties of green tea, resulting in an increased consumption of this beverage by people all over the world.*

Right: *Moxibustion is used by TCM doctors to heat pressure points, thus releasing the flow of qi within the body.*

Nowadays both in China and in the West, many doctors, practitioners and patients use TCM in conjunction with conventional biomedicine. Acupressure has even been used as an anesthetic during operations. Many who practice Traditional Chinese Medicine and Western medicine in conjunction believe these two, seemingly opposing philosophies and treatments of the body, are extremely complementary, providing many with the best possible outcomes for improved health.

Nearly all of 8,000 or so medicines used within TCM are extracted from plants, animals, or even minerals.

Left: *Various kinds of tea are used within Chinese Medicine because of its healing and restorative properties.*

Far Left: *Modern acupuncture needles like these are used to pierce the skin at various pressure points.*

Religion

Today, every major religion has a presence within the borders of China. Historically, however, China was home to three major schools of religious thought and practice: Confucianism, Daoism, and Buddhism. Confucianism, the oldest of the three, originated with the writings and ideology of Confucius, who lived from 551–479 BC. Daoism is perhaps known more for its philosophical traditions and concepts, which rely heavily on theories of the *Dao*, or the "way," and *yin* and *yang*. The main texts of Daoism include the *I Ching*, or the *Book of Changes* as well as the *Daode Jing*, said to be written by the founder of Daoism, Laozi. Buddhism's history in China is traced to the Silk Road, where it was brought over by traders and travelers from India. Often considered complementary rather than oppositional, these three religions continue to be practiced in tandem by the population of China.

Below: *The Temple of Heaven in Beijing was an important site for worship, prayer, and ritual for the emperor of China.*

Right: *The lotus flower is one of the many symbols of Buddhism.*

Confucianism is a school of thought that developed in China over thousands of years. It is attributed to the philosopher Confucius, who lived from 551–479 BC. Confucius' main concerns were with morality, the question of being and the values ascribed to both queries. Instituted by numerous dynasties throughout Chinese history, Confucianism played an immensely important role in the establishment of Chinese bureaucracy and institutions. The notion of filial piety is perhaps Confucius' most influential and lasting contribution to Chinese culture and society. Service, devotion, and obedience to one's parents, grandparents, and ancestors are the foundation of filial piety. This obedience is meant to extend out, beyond one's family to the ruler—namely, the emperor—of the nation. For Confucius, filial piety is the basis for society and, furthermore, of morality; this hierarchical relationship every member of society has with family, government and ancestors binds a nation, securing its respect for patriarchal order. Obedience and respect are at the core of filial piety, thus securing the order of the empire and maintenance of the masses. Respect for the authority of one's brothers, fathers, male ancestors and rulers is tantamount to securing harmony, stability and peace within a nation under Confucian philosophy. Filial piety is unarguably one of the most important principles within Chinese culture and forms the basis for the institution of the family for Chinese communities all over the world.

Along with Confucianism, Daoism is one of the two religions native to China. Laozi, the main figure associated with the founding of Daoism, lived sometime during the 6th century BC and is considered the author of the *Daode Jing*, the seminal text of Daoism. More popular among the common people than Confucianism, Daoism focused on individual freedoms as they applied to the *Dao*, or the "way." Confucianism's focus on filial piety and service to the emperor was used by dynasties to regulate their subjects. In contrast, Daoism's focus on self-intuition and self-governance, in accordance with the way and nature, relies far less on the notion of an external governing body. As long as people work in harmony with the *Dao*, the notion of government becomes superfluous.

Buddhism in China owes its beginnings and subsequent growth to the Silk Road. Namely used as a trade route between China and Western Asia and Europe, the Silk Road carried along it much more than goods to be traded or bartered. One of the most influential and lasting contributions the travelers along the Silk Road brought to China was Buddhism, carried over from India sometime in the 1st century AD. This famed trading route carried religious thought, doctrine, practices, and rituals for thousands of years, slowly changing along the way to create the Buddhism of China and Tibet. Following the Mahayana School of Buddhism, this branch emphasizes universal compassion and self-sacrifice in the pursuit of the "awakened mind." Buddhism bases its teachings on the Buddha, Siddhartha Gautama, who lived during the 6th century BC in northern India. Buddhism was particularly popular in China during times of crisis and disunity, when the tenets of Confucianism, which held up the authority of the emperor, were challenged. China has experienced several periods of both Buddhist revival and suppression, yet it has remained the most practiced religion in China.

One of the most influential and lasting contributions the travelers along the Silk Road brought to China was Buddhism, carried over from India sometime in the 1st century AD.

Left: *Confucian scholars, as depicted by these figurines, studied the teachings and sayings of Confucius.*

Below: *Huge joss sticks fill temples especially during holy times or festivals, like Chinese New Year.*

Unique to Chinese Buddhism is the image of the Maitreya Buddha, who is usually seated, laughing with his large belly protruding below him. Maitreya Buddha depicts the abundance and happiness that the Buddha offers to all who follow in his path to enlightenment.

Below: *The image of the rotund, laughing Buddha is a sign of prosperity and abundance.*

Right: *The Lion Dance is performed each New Year by skillful acrobats and dancers.*

The symbols and icons of Buddhism fill many temples, monasteries and homes in China. Most common are the various images of the Buddha himself, who may be represented as the jovial, rotund Buddha or as the seated, meditating Buddha. Unique to Chinese Buddhism is the image of the Maitreya Buddha, who is usually seated, laughing with his large belly protruding below him. This image depicts abundance and happiness that the Buddha offers to all who follow in his path to enlightenment. Different representations of the Buddha can be seen throughout China, in as diverse places as the historic cave paintings of Dunhuang, or on the lush Lantau Island of Hong Kong, or along the confluence of the Min, Dadu, and Qingyi Rivers in Sichuan province where the enormous 230-foot Great Buddha has been carved out of the side of a mountain. Nearly any visit to a Chinese city confirms the enormous importance that this religion has had on the history and culture of its people.

Like Buddhism, Islam's presence in China can be traced back to the Silk Road and probably entered China sometime during the 9th century. Making its way first through the present-day province of Xinjiang, Islam today is practiced by more than 13 million Chinese, with Muslims residing in nearly every province. A vast majority of the Muslim population within China belong to the *Hui* ethnic minority, who speak the Chinese language and are ethnically Chinese but are distinguished as a separate group due to religious and dietary differences. The second largest Muslim population within China are a mixture of several nationalities that, for the most part, live in the northwesternmost province of Xinjiang. Xinjiang is the largest of China's provinces, making up one-sixth of China's territory. Its predominant Uighur population are a Turkic-speaking people.

Islam, Buddhism, Daoism, and Confucianism are part and parcel of Chinese history. Today, much of China's population looks to these religions and the ideologies and philosophies they promote to gain an understanding of their culture and history. The banning of all religious thought and practice during the Cultural Revolution is evidence of the strength and tenacity of religious thought and belief among the Chinese people. Such long-held traditions, like the example of filial piety, have infused the Chinese culture so profoundly that even today the institution of the family remains at the core of Chinese society.

Left: *Meditation is an important aspect of the Buddhist faith.*

Right: *The image of the seated Buddha is ubiquitous throughout China.*

Shanghai

The skyline of Shanghai is one of the most striking in all of China. It is an architect's dream and a visual feast for any onlooker.

Shanghai is one of three autonomous municipalities in China and is China's most populated city, home to over 14 million citizens. It is one of the most densely populated regions in the world and, alongside Hong Kong, is one of China's major financial and economic hubs. Shanghai sits on the far eastern side of the country, where the Yangzi River flows out into the East China Sea. For this reason, Shanghai is a major port and even the name of this city—meaning "above the sea"—illustrates the importance both the river and the seaside have on this huge, pulsating metropolis.

Perhaps more so than any other mainland Chinese city, Shanghai has symbolized China's interest in, and compliance with, Western influence. Following the loss of the Opium Wars to Britain, China was forcefully persuaded to sign the Treaty of Nanjing, thus opening the ports of Guangzhou, Xiamen, Fuzhou, Ningbo and, most critically, Shanghai. The Treaty of Nanjing also ceded Hong Kong to Britain and created "concessions" for British, French, and American foreign residents of these port cities, demarcating certain areas where foreigners were answerable to the laws of their respective countries. During this period, Shanghai grew immensely and by 1900 had a population of one million.

It was during the decade between the 1920s and 1930s when Shanghai witnessed a transformation that brought it to worldly status of glamour and wealth. Various banks opened headquarters in Shanghai during this time, western-style architecture was erected, the first department stores in China were opened, and opium dens flourished alongside an underworld filled with gangsters, brothels, and gambling. Even today, the

Left: *Shanghai has long been a center of modernity and cosmopolitanism.*

Above: *The Shanghai skyline by night, with the Oriental Pearl TV Tower soaring high above the city.*

Above: *A common street scene where people meet to chat or drink tea on any given afternoon.*

Bund of Shanghai—a grand boulevard that runs alongside the Huangpu River and is lined with the European-style architecture typical of this era—represents this period of Shanghai's history and remains the main attraction of the city.

In the early twentieth century, Shanghai became home to thousands of refugees from Russia and various eastern European countries. Fleeing civil unrest in their home country, Russians began arriving in Shanghai as early as 1919 and became, after the Japanese, the second-largest foreign community within the city. During World War II, Jews fled from Europe into Shanghai. It is estimated that nearly 32,000 Jews settled in Shanghai during the Second World War.

The skyline of Shanghai is one of the most striking in all of China, including European promenades like the Bund, modern skyscrapers of the Pudong area that sit just opposite the Bund along the Huangpu River, and the gardens and pavilions of the Ming dynasty that can be found in the center of the city. It is an architect's dream and a visual feast for any onlooker. Of the modern buildings that fill the economic zone of Pudong, the outline of the Oriental Pearl TV Tower is unmistakable. Standing at 1,500 feet and home to the Shanghai History Museum, the Pearl Tower sits in the center of one of the world's largest building sites whose completed high-rises are, ironically, 70% empty due to plummeting property prices. The Oriental Pearl TV Tower is China's largest structure and looms over China's tallest skyscraper, the Jinmao Dasha Building.

In the mid-sixteenth century, the then-governor of Sichuan Province built the Yu Gardens that are now home to several teahouses, a bustling shopping area,

In the early twentieth century, Shanghai became home to thousands of refugees from Russia fleeing civil unrest in their home country.

Below: *One of the many stalls selling dolls depicting various ethnic minorities at Yu Gardens in Shanghai.*

restaurants with local delicacies, as well as the gardens that were the original intention of Governor Yu. Much like a bazaar, Yu Gardens is packed with vendors and buyers during the summer months and over the weekends all year round. Strolling around the shops, it would seem that anything under the sun could be purchased here, and it very well may be true. Tea, traditional medicinal cures, firecrackers, clothing, swords, pearls, scrolls, toys, and carved pipes are just some of the items that are bargained over in this hectic but ever-alluring marketplace.

Like most large cities within China, Shanghai is experiencing a period of rapid growth, continued modernization and development. In October 2010, Shanghai will host the Expo 2010, a World's Fair whose slogan is "Better City—Better Life." The Expo will mark Shanghai's emergence as a cultural and economic center in the 21st century. Shanghai is also home to the world's first commercially run Maglev train, a magnetically powered, high-speed train. The train currently travels between Shanghai's Pudong International Airport and the city center, reaching speeds of up to 267 mph (431 km/h).

Perhaps more than any other Chinese city, Shanghai embodies an urbane, cosmopolitan style and way of life. It has been, and to a large extent continues to be, the center of art, architecture, and culture in China. While many ascribe this to the long-standing Western presence within the city, Shanghai has become a center for arts and culture in its own right. For visitors to this, the largest city in China, it becomes impossible to ignore the convergence of East and West. Whether visiting the Bund, Yu Gardens, or the Pudong economic zone, one is reminded of Shanghai's long history as a major international center where artists, bankers, refugees, tourists and aristocrats have come in search of its aesthetic delights.

Below: *Gang Hui Square, Shanghai.*

Above: *Yu Gardens, Shanghai.*

Architecture

Ranging from the pagodas of the Ming dynasty, to the grand palaces that housed the numerous emperors of China and the high rise buildings in Shanghai and Hong Kong, China's architecture is a vast mixture of styles: old and new, traditional and modern. The architecture of China spans over several eras and encompasses several distinct styles, many of which employ the philosophy of *feng shui* in layout and design.

The earliest buildings in China were made of wood, the oldest of which dates to 7,000 years ago in Zhejiang province. Architecture in China began much earlier than its first wooden structures, however, as there is evidence of earthen walls, palaces, foundations and tombs as early as the 21st century BC. The oldest known palace to date was found in Henan province and dates to the Shang dynasty, sometime during the 16th century BC. From an early date, two central features of Chinese architecture—the use of non-weight-bearing walls and a roof with large overhanging eaves—were shared by palaces, religious structures, halls, and even common houses alike. Most of these buildings also shared the feature of a central courtyard, whose outer buildings enclosed this private unroofed area. What this means for the architecture of China is that almost all buildings, regardless of their purpose or function, all share the same principles of construction and design. In this way, a palace is only a larger, more elaborate and expensive version of a common courtyard house.

The typical courtyard house utilizes the principles of *feng shui* for its layout and design. Ideally, the front door should be positioned along the southern wall of the courtyard, with the residences of the head of the family at the north end of the

Left: *The spectacular interior of Shanghai's Jinmao Dasha building.*

Below: *The Jinmao Dasha Building is one of China's tallest buildings.*

Above: *The Temple of Heaven in Beijing is an example of a Chinese pagoda.*

Left: *The geometrical Lippo Tower is just one of many skyscrapers in Hong Kong's modern business district.*

building. The number of halls a typical residence would have would depend largely on the social and economic status of its owners. These halls, big or small, many or few, would run along the west and east walls of the courtyard, often housing the younger brothers and their families. Near the entrance along the southern wall was where the servants of the household were quartered.

This north-south axis that every building in traditional China was based on is determined by the rules of geomancy, or *feng shui* in Chinese. Based on theories of *yin* and *yang*, *feng shui* aims to achieve balance within any given setting where human design is

Within feng shui, *the triangle is the most inauspicious shape. Its harsh angles pierce downward and threaten those found on any side of its injurious energy.*

involved. This means that in addition to palaces, homes and buildings, the principles of *feng shui* are also used in the construction of gravesites, gardens, entire cities and even the furnishings placed inside private and public buildings. Dating back to the Han dynasty, geomancy in China considers the energy of space and orders it in such a way as to produce harmony and balance for its residents and occupants.

Within *feng shui*, the triangle is the most inauspicious shape. Its harsh angles, it is thought, pierce downward, threatening those found on any side of its injurious energy. In general, both straight and sharp angles are to be avoided, as they are seen to be associated with evil and negativity. Within China, the association of the number four with ominous portents is due to its phonetic similarity to the Chinese word for death. In many

The outlawing of feng shui by the People's Republic of China has had little effect on the construction of many modern buildings, especially in Hong Kong.

Left: *An example of some of the Western-influenced apartment buildings that are being built throughout China.*

Below: *Typical housing built during the Ming dynasty.*

Chinese buildings, the fourth floor (like the 13th in the Western world) is omitted from numbering systems. Within a home or building, furniture should not be facing the door of the room in which it sits, but instead, if possible, should face water. Colors also play an important role in the layout and design of a room, red being the luckiest of all the colors.

The outlawing of *feng shui* by the People's Republic of China has had little effect on the construction of many modern buildings, especially in Hong Kong. The most famous of which is the Bank of China building, whose internationally acclaimed architect, I.M. Pei, ignored all principles of *feng shui* for its design. Considered extremely unlucky and envisioned as a giant Praying Mantis about to strike violently down on its occupants, Hong Kong residents often compare this building unfavorably against the widely loved HSBC building, whose British architect Sir Norman Foster closely followed *feng shui* guidelines.

The erection of palaces and temples follows the same guidelines and principles of *feng shui*. The most revered examples of architecture that successfully employs the balance and harmony sought by feng shui can be found at the Forbidden Palace and at the Temple of Heaven, or Tian Tan, in Beijing. Astounding in its symmetry, the Forbidden Palace utilizes the elements of water, stone, and wood as well as carefully placed colors to bring about specific protections, good fortunes or to ward away certain deities. Numbers also play an

Left: *Typical architecture found along the canal cities of southern China.*

Right: *The grand and austere architecture of the Summer Palace.*

important and specific role in the design of any palace, home, or temple. Within the Forbidden City, numbers of rooms, lions guarding the palace, studs on doors and even the number of guardian figures placed on rooftops follow specific principles according to *yin* and *yang* elements. For example, odd numbers represent *yang* elements, whereas even numbers represent *yin*. Because the ruler of the kingdom, and hence the Forbidden City, is typically a male emperor, many of the features within the imperial palace are placed in odd numbers. Rumored to have 9,999 rooms, the Forbidden Palace exemplifies *yang* essence, but with balancing *yin* elements like water and various royal gardens.

The Temple of Heaven—Tian Tan—in Beijing is a religious complex that was built during the Ming dynasty. Filled with symbols, Tian Tan was used by the emperor for religious, sacrificial, and ritual purposes. It was not a site meant for commoners and was closed to much of the public during Ming and Qing times. The largest of the temples at Tian Tan is the Qinian Dian, a 125-foot high, round building with a tiled roof and an ornately painted interior. This is where the emperor would pray to the gods, worship his ancestors, and make symbolic offerings. The Tian Tan site also contains an expansive marble platform decorated in numerous dragons, a round altar site and the Imperial Vault of Heaven. Peaceful, colorful and grand, the Temple of Heaven is one of China's many architectural treasures.

Left: *The octagonal pagoda, such as this one, derives from Tantric Buddhism, which considers the number eight to be most auspicious.*

Right: *The modern skyline of Qingdao, China.*

Common to most temples in China, the pagoda is a tall tower that originated as the stupa in India. The *stupa* traveled, along with Buddhism, the Silk Road and variations of this tall, multi-tiered structure can be seen as it spread throughout China. The typical Indian Buddhist stupa was designed to house important texts and relics of the religion. Traditional Tibetan stupas are closer in design and stature to their Indian counterparts. Typically round with a square base and colored white, Tibetan stupas paved the way for the pagoda of later dynasties in China. The earliest known pagoda of China sat in Henan province, where the 449-foot (137 m) Yongning Temple made entirely of wood dated to 516 AD. Today, the oldest pagoda still standing can be found in Shanxi province. Standing at 221 feet (67 m), this wooden building was erected in 1056 and is an example of the octagonal pagoda, referred to as the Sakyamuni Pagoda, that was popular during its time. The Temple of Heaven in Beijing is more recent example of a pagoda, whose main round building uses several of the key features to pagoda-style architecture: several tiered roofs that taper as they ascend in height, the use of pillars and the spike placed at the very top of the structure, often in the shape of a lotus bud.

Left: *The houses of China are suited to the landscape in which they are found.*

Right: *This Beijing watchtower is some of the last remaining evidence of the original defensive walls built around Beijing. Today, the southeast tower is home to the Red Gate Gallery that houses modern Chinese art.*

Architecture since the 1950s in China has largely been in the Soviet Communist style, whose concrete block buildings are common in Beijing. Today, much of Chinese architecture looks to the West for design inspiration. Western skylines reminiscent of New York are popping up in Shanghai, Hong Kong and even Beijing, as old buildings come down to make way for the their shiny new replacements. Not far from these massive, modern complexes, however, are the temples, pagodas, courtyard homes and palaces typical of traditional Chinese architecture.

Left: *The expanse and grandeur of the Great Wall of China is an architectural marvel.*

Above: *Riverside housing outside the city of Shanghai.*

Traditional and Modern Arts

The arts of China have a long and distinguished history. The traditional arts of China include pottery, painting, lacquerware, calligraphy, textiles, and sculpture. Many of these arts take the form of religious works, particularly sculpture and painting. Some of the earliest arts of China are Buddhist paintings and sculptures discovered along the Silk Road.

The most famous of Buddhist paintings in China lie in the caves of Dunhuang in the Taklamakan Desert in the western province of Gansu. The site of Dunhuang is the oldest Buddhist site in all of China and the paintings found inside the caves are considered among the world's most important Buddhist works of art. It took monks over 700 years to complete the paintings that can be viewed today, whose influences range from India and central Asia. The cave paintings at Dunhuang were completed between the 4th and 11th centuries AD. The Dunhuang caves are also where the oldest printed book, the Buddhist scripture of the *Diamond Sutra*, was discovered in the early twentieth century.

The Silk Road influenced other works of art in China, including those made of gold and silver, which were, before their introduction, largely ignored in value or status. During the Tang dynasty, however, both of these precious metals became popular in the production of cups, vases, and bowls as prized items for trade. The Silk Road owes its name to China's greatest export and most sought after commodity: silk. It was the wife of the legendary Yellow Emperor who discovered, while sitting under a tree, the production of silk cocoons by worms. She then learned how to farm the worms to extract their silk, finally weaving it into fabric. Since then, silk has

Left: *Ancient stone carvings can be found at religious shrines and temples. They demonstrate the importance of religion within the art of China.*

Right: *Antique woodwork is one of the many traditional art forms of China.*

been the foundation of perhaps the most important industry throughout China's history. For much of this period, China held the secrets of silk production, thus creating a global monopoly on this sought-after material. Originally limited to the use and wear of the Imperial court, silk was regarded as *the* cloth of the powerful. These silk items of clothing were elaborately embroidered with various important symbols, some of which include mountains and waves, the dragon, the axe, or the double chi—an important symbol delineating the emperor from others who may have worn these prized silk robes.

One of China's greatest inventions is also one of its greatest art forms: porcelain. Years of refinement and cultivation led to China's first production of porcelain in approximately 600 AD, during the Sui dynasty. Each dynasty thereafter improved and developed upon the art of porcelain. The Han dynasty is known for its advancement in glazing, where pots truly became works of art. The tri-colored porcelain is attributed to the Tang dynasty, the Song for its simplicity and for the development of the "cracked" technique. The Yuan's blue and white porcelain paved the way for the extraordinary pottery of the Ming dynasty. Ming porcelain remains the most sought-after and highly prized pottery to come out of China. Its intricate blue and white designs often feature dynamic floral designs. Hugely influencing the pottery and porcelain of Europe, the porcelain of China is yet another important product of this country.

Silk, bamboo or paper is traditionally used as the canvas of Chinese paintings, whose most famous genres include landscape and religious subjects. The subjects of landscape painting range from the famous bird-and-flower styles to the "mountains and water" style that the name of landscape painting in Chinese, *shanshuihua*, refers to. These types of landscape paintings were often considered a relative of calligraphy, which also used ink on paper and similar methods in strokes and application of ink. Bird-and-flower painting, by contrast, was a

Below: *Symbolizing longevity, jade is carved into jewelry, vases, boxes, and amulets.*

Right: *Calligraphy often accompanies ink paintings in China. The crane is an important figure within traditional Bird-and-Flower paintings.*

medium used by Chinese Daoists, whose love of nature could be depicted in such paintings. Often symbolizing freedom and spiritual awakening, the most popular birds depicted in these paintings include geese and nightingales.

The arts in China suffered greatly during the Cultural Revolution, when traditional art forms were banned, denounced, and destroyed. Many artists during this time went into hiding, fearful of persecution and abuse that the Red Guard inflicted upon any who were perceived as promoting "old" ways. Stories of musicians and artists hiding instruments, paintings, sculpture, and anything else that might be in danger of destruction were common. The Naxi of the southwest province of Yunnan were among those who buried their beloved instruments in fear of destruction. Years later, well after the threat that the Cultural Revolution posed to artists was over, the Naxi dug up their instruments and began playing once again. Today, in the ancient city of Lijiang that is home to the Naxi people, those who remember the time when their music went silent teach the children and youth how to play the music of their culture. This effort has developed into the Naxi Music Academy, whose nightly performances display their unique music that combines Confucian and Daoist musical traditions.

Greater contact with the West has also influenced the arts of China. Though much of China's arts suffered during the mid- to late-twentieth century, contemporary art in China since the 1990s has been undergoing a massive regeneration and, to some extent, revolution. New schools and trends in art were established in China, such as the Cynical Realism School founded by artist Fang Lijun. Many of these works were produced in response to the 1989 demonstrations at Tian'an Men Square. Grappling with questions about modernity, globalization, and transnational identity, the contemporary arts of China are groundbreaking, unparalleled and highly influential within today's artistic climate.

One of China's greatest inventions is also one of its greatest art forms: porcelain. The first glazed pots to be fired in a kiln date back to the Shang dynasty of around 1500 BC.

Left: *A stone carving depicting the Forbidden City.*

Below: *The elephant is an important animal to the Dai people of the southern province of Yunnan.*

Beijing Opera

Opera within China is a long-held tradition that has been popular in several provinces, each with its own version of this theatrical art form. There are a total of 365 different styles of opera that exist throughout China, from various regions and provinces. The music of the opera employs various stringed instruments, including the *erhu* and the *huqin*, which are two-stringed fiddles, and the *yueqin*, an oval-shaped guitar. Percussion is also used in the music of Chinese opera in the form of gongs and clappers. Other instruments include various pipes, lutes, and Chinese horns. Perhaps the most famous of all styles and regions of opera is the Beijing Opera, whose beginnings date to the Qing dynasty. Many of the Qing emperors, including the Empress Dowager Cixi, were fans of the opera. It was Emperor Qianlong who brought the opera to Beijing from the provinces of Hebei and Anhui, where a distinctive style of music, costume and dance had flourished throughout the previous years. Another renowned style of opera in China comes from the Sichuan province of southwestern China. Sichuan Opera is a more informal affair and often is held in large auditoriums. Children may be left to play outside while grandparents sit in, eating seeds and nuts, watching the elaborately costumed singers and performers.

Beijing Opera is distinguished from other styles in China by its use of all the elements of traditional Chinese opera: singing, mime, acrobatics, speech, and visual effects. Within Beijing Opera and other opera styles throughout China, there are four main roles that are depicted: the *sheng*, or male, role who can be young or old and is depicted with subdued makeup; the *dan*, or female, role of which there are a total of six types ranging in age and virtue; the *jing*, or "painted face," roles are more flamboyant, who may be depicted in such favorite characters as monkeys, heroes, warriors

Right: *The* sheng *(man) and* dan *(female) characters within Beijing opera wear more naturalistic makeup, colorful costumes, and elaborate headdresses.*

or even demons; the *chou* are the jesters of the production, who may or may not wear a mask. One of the most famous and renowned arts of China, the Beijing Opera has stood the test of time. As one of the "four olds" attacked during the Cultural Revolution, the Beijing Opera suffered during the twentieth century. Many of the opera houses were closed or burned, and the intricate costumes and masks the artists wore were destroyed. Its resiliency and popularity through to today has proven the Beijing Opera to be a lasting contribution to Chinese culture. The artistry and skill of the Beijing Opera amazes all who go to see this theatrical production.

Below: *Some of the many masks worn in the various styles of Chinese opera.*

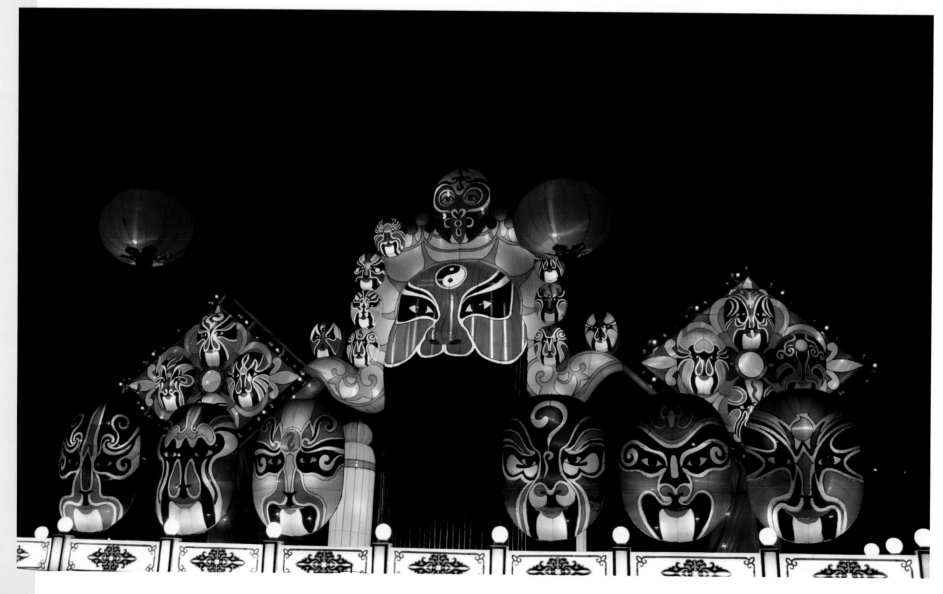

Writing and Calligraphy

Proof of the importance of the written word in China is evidenced by one word used to encompass two phenomena: the term for "civilization" and the term for "script" are described by the same word, *wen*. Originating with ideographs, the characters that comprise the Chinese language began as images etched onto shells and bones. These writings are the earliest archaeological records of the Chinese language, known as the oracle bones of the Shang dynasty, dating from around 1300 BC. Over time, characters were added to the language culminating in over 60,000 characters that comprise the Chinese language of today. Traditionally, Chinese is read from top to bottom, right to left. Since the 1950s the Pinyin system of Romanization has been used in China to make Chinese words legible to speakers of other languages. Simplification of Chinese characters, separating a more traditional form of writing from a more modern one, has been implemented by the government and spread down through the school system. Though spoken Chinese varies immensely from region to region and from province to province, all share the written form of Mandarin and thus can, to some extent, communicate on this basis.

The Chinese art of writing, known as calligraphy, is one of the great arts of China and has been in practice since the invention of paper, between 100 and 200 AD. Deemed just as intricate and involving just as much skill as painting, poetry or sculpture, calligraphy is an art form that one learns and begins to practice from a very young age in China. The art of calligraphy, it is thought, represents the spiritual and moral qualities of the scribe through his interpretation of the characters depicted.

Above: *Ink seals such as these typically contain the name of the artist.*

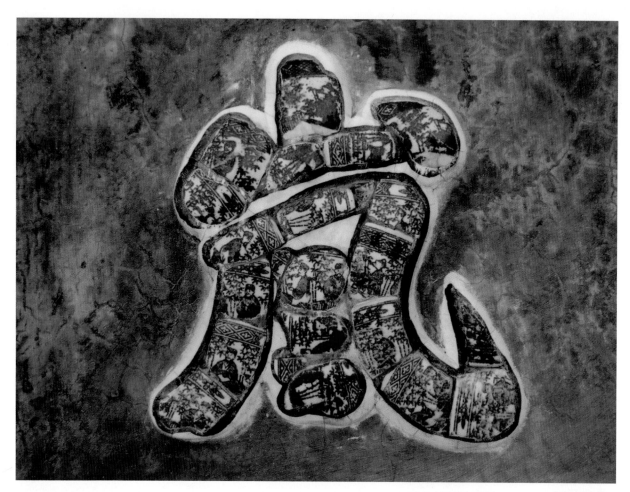

Printing was invented in China and after the invention of paper in approximately 104 AD, various texts and books were available for mass production. The world's earliest complete, printed book, the Buddhist *Diamond Sutra*, dates to 868 AD. China's printing technology predates European efforts, who began printing and developing movable type 400–600 years after the Chinese. Though the Chinese were the first to develop and implement movable type, the nature of the Chinese language did not permit this process to be an easy or quick one. Such an effort would require the production, use, and realignment of several thousand pieces for a mere few pages of type.

There are six major types of calligraphy: Zhuanshu, Lishu, Kaishu, Cao Shu, Xingshu, and finally the simplified script initiated by Mao Zedong. The first style, Zhuanshu, is the seal script used during ancient times and was developed during the Zhou dynasty. This style tends to be heavier in brush stroke than any of the subsequent styles. The second, Lishu, was developed during Han times and is considered a clerical and official script. Regarded as the most important of all the styles, the Lishu style is also the most complicated of all the calligraphic types because of its use of all the brush strokes possible. Connected to the Lishu style, Kaishu is considered the "regular" style of Chinese script and it is this style that is taught in schools all across the country. Cao Shu, literally meaning "grass

Above Left: *An example of thick-style calligraphy.*

Below Left: *This China press sign demonstrates the varying styles of calligraphy seen within today's print media.*

script," is known for its abstract, cursive and abbreviated style. Cao Shu is often limited to those artists who have studied the art of calligraphy for many years. The last of the artistic styles, Xingshu is also called "running script" because the characters tend to bleed together when written. This is the style that most letters and personal correspondence are written in.

The criteria by which calligraphy is measured lie largely within the individual brush strokes that make up a character. Performed in a specific order, each stroke within a given character has eight possible styles. Angle and weight given to any number of strokes dramatically changes the look and feel of a character, giving some lines a heavy or light look, while others may be tapered and lighter in width. A skillful artist will give each composition a look and feel of balance and liveliness. Upon judging a work, four criteria are considered: strength of the lines (referred to as the "bone" quality of the stroke due to its unbreakable quality), appearance of a stroke that is abundant but not over-fed (referred to as the "flesh" of the mark), the connection between strokes (the "muscle"), and finally the quality of the ink (the "blood" of the image, whose consistency should not be watery yet not too viscous). The metaphor of the body is used in judging calligraphy. Indeed, for the work to be considered of high form and value, it must move like a living thing, embody balance, and have an organic quality.

Buddha **Zen**

Law **Tao**

Above: *Each stroke within a character can be highly stylized, demarcating a particular artist's craftsmanship.*

The metaphor of the body is used in judging calligraphy. Indeed, for the work to be considered of high form and value, it must move like a living thing, embody balance, and have an organic quality.

Hong Kong

Hong Kong is one of the largest duty-free ports in the world and follows only New York and London as a world financial center.

Returned in 1997 to China after over 150 years of British rule inaugurated by the signing of the Treaty of Nanjing, Hong Kong is a dense amalgamation of British and Cantonese culture. Hong Kong is home to lavish malls, double-decker buses, traditional temples, typical southern markets and the world's third-largest producer of motion pictures, following Bollywood of India and Hollywood. Hong Kong is often considered the New York of Asia because of its spectacularly dense downtown and grandiose skyline, filled with the modern bank buildings that dominate the financial sectors of China. Surrounding Hong Kong's financial centers and apartment high rises are lush, green hills, fed by the subtropical weather that Hong Kong benefits from. Nearly all of Hong Kong's population of almost 7 million lives on only 15 percent of the land area, largely due to its mountainous terrain. Yet, Hong Kong remains one of the most densely populated cities in the world. This could be, in part, due to the fact that less than 25 percent of the land area of Hong Kong is developed. Separated by Victoria Harbor, Hong Kong is divided between Kowloon to the south and Hong Kong Island to the north. More than 230 islands dot the South China Sea that borders Hong Kong, the largest of which is Lantau Island, home to the world's largest bronze statue of the seated Buddha.

Left: *Hong Kong at dusk.*

Above: *The busy streets of Hong Kong are a colorful amalgamation of western and Chinese cultures.*

Hong Kong is one of the largest duty-free ports in the world and follows only New York and London as a world financial center. Now considered part of the PRC, Hong Kong is still separated from the mainland by its currency and economics. China has deemed Hong Kong a Special Administrative Region in order that it maintains its economic autonomy. Much of Hong Kong's development is, relatively speaking, fairly new. The skyline that gives Hong Kong its modern grandeur today only began to appear in the 1980s and 1990s, in the decade before Britain's handover of the region back to Chinese rule.

Towering over the city with breathtaking views of the harbor stands Victoria Peak. As the premier place to reside in the mid-nineteenth century, many of the former colonial aristocracy of Hong Kong lived on Victoria Peak and, for many years, Chinese were banned from owning property here. Today, it is the most sought-after location to buy a home in Hong Kong and the properties on Victoria Peak rank among the priciest in the world.

Hong Kong's film industry is one of the largest in the world. Unlike its Western counterpart, the films of Hong Kong receive little to no money from government subsidies and therefore rely almost exclusively on their commercial success. Kung Fu, or *gong fu* in Chinese, has become synonymous with Hong Kong film, with international stars such as Jet Li, Bruce Lee, and Jackie Chan leading the pack of stars to come out of this genre. Pared down and simplified to fit within the plot and to make the movements seem realistic, the *gong fu* of film is much different from its real-life version. There are several schools of *gong fu*, ranging from those that more closely resemble a meditative art

Now considered part of the People's Republic of China, Hong Kong is still separated from the mainland by its currency and economics.

Left: *Hong Kong by night.*

Below: *The bright neon lights of Hong Kong's nightlife.*

to those that incorporate various weapons. Though Hong Kong's kung fu films have perhaps been the most popular of the films to come out of southern China, other directors and artists have risen to international acclaim. The films of Wong Kar Wai, in particular, have gained critical acclaim and success abroad, garnering nominations and awards in various international ceremonies.

Macau sits roughly 45 miles (72 km) west of Hong Kong, across the South China Sea. The first European settlement in China, Macau was first visited by Portuguese traders in the early 1500s and became a colony of Portugal in 1557. Portugal ruled over Macau for 450 years and was a vibrant gambling

Below: *The enormous bronze Buddha of Lantau Island.*

Right: *A bustling Hong Kong street scene.*

center during World War II. Even today, Macau is a huge gambling center within southern China, where horse and greyhound racing, an annual Grand Prix and several ritzy casinos operate. Today, Macau's quaint and colorful colonial buildings in addition to the unique hybrid of Chinese and Portuguese cuisine are what attract tourists to this postcolonial city. Together, Macau and Hong Kong are two of China's heavily westernized cities, whose cultures over time have culminated in unique amalgamations of southern Chinese, British, and Portuguese influences.

Left: *One of the many ferries that cross Victoria Harbor each day.*

Below: *The wave-like roof of Hong Kong's Convention and Exhibition Center is one of the many unmistakable buildings of this southern city.*

Festivals continue to hold a significant place in Chinese culture and history and are still practiced in varying degrees by Chinese all over the world.

Below: *The vivid neon lights that fill the cities of China during Spring Festival.*

Right: *Chinese New Year fireworks as seen from across Victoria Harbor.*

Festivals

Festivals remain an important aspect of Chinese life. Typically times thought to bring good luck, prosperity, fortune and harmony to home and family life, the traditional festivals of China are vibrant, boisterous, joyous days. Tied to various legends and stories, most Chinese festivals are connected to the farming seasons and the lunar cycle. Festivals, on the whole, continue to hold a significant place in Chinese culture and history and are still practiced in varying degrees by Chinese all over the world. Spring Festival (*Chun Jie*), or Chinese New Year as it is known in the West, is the most important of the yearly festivals and is celebrated every year all across the globe with huge parades and firework shows taking place in cities such as San Francisco, London, and New York.

As the beginning to the Chinese New Year, Spring Festival commences with the settling of debts and the cleaning of houses. As it is considered unlucky to have any old business or clutter follow from the old year to the new, much effort is made during the months of December and January to reconcile books and statements and to wipe away the dust that has settled in months past. House cleaning is especially important during this time, as it is believed that the Kitchen God travels from Earth to Heaven to make his annual report. As the most important deity that presides over the family and home, several rituals and traditions surround the legend of the Kitchen God. While the Kitchen God is an important feature all year within a Chinese household, the New Year is especially significant with regard to pleasing the Kitchen God. In an effort to gain the Kitchen God's good favor, families clean and make offerings to him and, on New Year's Eve, erect a new picture of him

above the stove. In order to ensure that the Kitchen God has nothing but sweet things to say about one's family while in heaven, his mouth is smeared with honey in the weeks before Spring Festival. It is this time when he temporarily departs from earth and the stove he guards. His return, marked by the new picture placed above the stove, announces the coming of the New Year, after which several special dishes are prepared for the traditional New Year's feast that takes place among family members.

The legend of Spring Festival is said to date back to ancient times. A wild beast, called *nian* (meaning "year" in Chinese), marauded through the same village year after year in the winter months, eating anyone who came in his path. In an attempt to drive *nian* away, the people of the village began setting off firecrackers, loudly beating on drums and gongs and performing a dance in the disguise of a lion. In general, the noise associated with the New Year that comes in the form of drumming or firecrackers is meant to drive away any evil spirit. Red is the color of the New Year, with paper money, door scrolls, lanterns, and candy wrappers all bathed in this color, meant to symbolize anything that is associated with good luck or happiness. Tangerines, a symbol of good luck, and flowers, symbolizing new beginnings, can be found in homes and restaurants during the New Year festivities. Foods such as fish, pork, dumplings, and lichees are all thought to bring specific fortunes associated with them.

Lion dances are performed every New Year, usually by dancers or acrobats who wear a lion-costume and put on an amazing display of agility and skill. The lion, whose ferocity and menacing character was thought to be no match for the beast *nian*, is often

Left: *Dancers dressed in costume for one of the many Chinese New Year dances performed in the streets.*

Below: *Typical Chinese New Year decorations.*

represented within China as a mix between a dog and a lion. The Lion costume that is worn by dancers has gold eyes and silver teeth, threatening the people along the street whom he comes into contact with. The Lion can only be appeased by the gift of money or coins. As a symbol of power and strength, a pair of lions can almost always be found at the entrance to most palaces and temples, the most famous of which sit at the gates of the Forbidden Palace.

The Lantern Festival that falls 15 days after the start of the New Year marks the close of Spring Festival. Paper lanterns are made in the shapes of all kinds of animals, typically those thought to bear auspicious meanings, such as dragons, birds, monkeys, or fish. The Lantern Festival dates to the Han dynasty (206 BC-220 AD) and is accompanied by foods such as sticky rice balls and taro root. Lanterns are an important fixture to any large and important celebration, not merely relegated to the Lantern Festival. On wedding days, birthdays, even national holidays such as May Day and National Day, lanterns can be seen hanging on the outside of a family gate, in the halls of restaurants and hotels and even in the squares and along the main boulevards of a city. They symbolize knowledge and are thought to guide the souls of ancestors from earth back to heaven.

Left: *Hand painted lanterns like these are hung during the Lantern Festival, marking the close of the New Year celebrations.*

Right: *To the Chinese, red is the most auspicious of all the colors. Many offices, hotels, and restaurants are decorated in red to bring fortune and good luck.*

The Dragon Boat Festival in June is most popular in southern China, where boats compete in races just outside the city of Guangzhou. Traditionally, the dragon is the overseer of the waterways and of the rainy season in China; the Dragon Boat Festival was a time to please this mythical beast in order to bring about the water necessary for an abundant growing season. The boats used during the Dragon Boat Festivals in southern China are typically long and narrow, adorned with dragons and painted to look like this mythical beast. Dragons within China, however, are mostly viewed as benign creatures that have enormous powers over the fertility of the earth as well as human fertility.

Often a symbol of purity and tranquility, the lotus flower is a recurring motif in Chinese Buddhism and appears frequently in traditional arts, particularly in ceramics and lacquered panels. The sixth moon in the lunar calendar is associated with the lotus flower, a time when late summer rains provide the water necessary for a successful harvest season. Within Buddhism, the lotus flower is linked to the Lotus Sutra, perhaps the most important scripture within the Buddhist religion, proclaiming the opportunity of all mankind to attain enlightenment. The lotus flower, which begins its growth in the thick mud of ponds and pools, sprouts up through the water, finally reaching the surface where it opens facing the sun, is symbolically compared to the trials and suffering that all face during life. And, like the flower, according to the principles of Mahayana Buddhism, truth can rise out of evil, just as man has the ability to rise out of the world of suffering in search of enlightenment.

Left: *The sixth moon in the lunar calendar is associated with the lotus flower.*

Below: *Dragons are believed to be the guardians of many of China's waterways and of its rainfall. The rituals of the Dragon Boat Festival are meant to bring about good luck in the coming rainy season.*

Dragons within China are viewed as benign creatures that have enormous powers over the fertility of the earth as well as human fertility.

Below: *Lion masks are worn by performers during the famous Lion Dance that takes place during New Year celebrations.*

Right: *Many take part in the Dragon Dance, unlike the Lion Dance which is performed by a select few with well-honed acrobatic skills.*

The Mid-Autumn Festival, also known as the Moon Festival or even the Autumn Moon Festival, takes place in the 8th lunar month, usually falling in the middle of September, celebrates the harvest moon. Sweet, round cakes filled with different pastes, called mooncakes, are eaten during this time. As a symbol of fertility and abundance, the moon is also associated with female, or *yin*, properties. Whereas the sun symbolizes the Emperor, the moon represents the Empress. During the Mid-Autumn Festival, children carry lanterns, families gather at night to view the full moon, and mirrors symbolizing the brightness of the moon are traditionally given as gifts.

Since 1949, China has adopted several national holidays that are associated with the founding of the Communist Party, such as National Day on October 1st, May Day on the first day of the month, and Women's Day on March 8th. The most important of these is unarguably National Day, marking the founding of the People's Republic of China by Mao Zedong in 1949. Celebrations are held for the entire first week of October and are a popular time for travel. These holidays, combined with the traditional festivals of China, serve as important times of year for the Chinese population all over the world. From the Spring Festival that heralds the beginning of the Chinese New Year to the Mid-Autumn Festival that pays special tribute to the moon, each festival in China is associated with particular deities and legends. Far from being relics of the past, these festivals are still a significant aspect to modern Chinese culture. More than anything else, they are times when families gather, give thanks and blessings for good luck and are filled with a host of special foods, dances, rituals and costumes.

Land

The geography of China is a vast, diverse terrain. The landscape and wildlife of this enormous country changes dramatically from region to region, making it one of the most ecologically interesting countries on the planet. From the Tibetan Plateau to the deserts of the north, the people who live in China have learned to adjust to their surroundings over the past several thousand years.

Below: *Fruits and vegetables grow in great abundance alongside China's rivers, where mineral-rich soil is found.*

Right: *The beautiful terraced rice fields of Guilin in southern China*

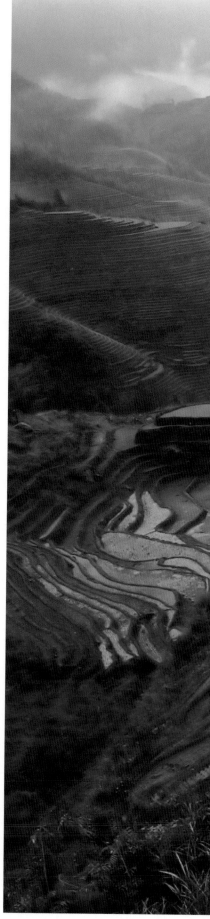

Left: *The limestone karst landscape is unique to Guilin and is one of China's many geographic wonders.*

Below: *Native only to China, the Giant Panda remains seriously in danger of extinction.*

China is home to more than 50,000 rivers. China's most important river, the Yangzi, is also the world's third-largest river. This massive flow of water spans a total of 3,915 miles (6300 km) from the mountains of Qinghai, covering 20 percent of China's total land area, finally reaching its end into the East China Sea at the port of Shanghai. The Three Gorges Dam, due to be completed in 2009, sits on the Yangzi River in western Hubei and will be the largest dam in the world. The dam is intended to provide hydroelectric energy to much of China. Yet, despite the economic benefits the country may gain from the harnessing of the Yangzi, the Three Gorges Dam will also force thousands of Chinese to relocate and cause immense environmental damage to animals and the flora and fauna of the region.

Equally important to Chinese culture, history and agriculture is the Yellow River, China's second-largest river at 3,400 miles (5472 km). Known as Huang He in Chinese, the Yellow River is regarded as "China's Sorrow" because of the disasters that have resulted from the frequent flooding and complete change of course this massive river undergoes. Enriching the soil with the silt the river produces, many of China's oldest civilizations and most fertile farming land can be found in the areas surrounding the Yellow River.

One third of China's landmass is covered in mountain ranges. Nine of China's highest peaks reach over 26,000 feet (7925 m) in height, ranking them among the tallest mountains in the entire world. The highest of these is Mount Everest, also the tallest peak in the world at 29,028 feet (8848 m), and is part of the Himalayas, which border Tibet and Nepal.

Fourteen countries border the 9.6 million square miles that comprise the People's Republic of China. China is also bordered by an expansive 12,400-mile (19,955 km)

Below: *Lying below the karst mountains of Guilin are massive cave systems.*

Right: *Rural China is covered with the lush green hues of the natural landscape.*

coastline, which runs along the eastern, southeastern and southern borders of the country. While China is home to 20 percent of the planet's population, only about 35 percent of its land mass is inhabited. The other 65 percent of China's land is home to some of the world's highest peaks and mountain ranges, making these regions a challenge for humans to live in.

Left: *The Stone Forest of Yunnan province.*

Below: *Snow-capped Yulong Mountain Range is one of Yunnan's many natural features.*

China is home to more than 50,000 rivers. China's most important river, the Yangzi, is also the world's third-largest river.

People

From the 1950s through to the 1970s, China underwent various Nationalities Identification Projects. During this time, the notion of an "ethnic minority" of China emerged. The government set criteria for this category and in order to be counted as an ethnic minority, a group must have the following in common: territory, language, an economy, and a binding "psychological" nature. The rationale for such a project was that, rather than ignore differences between groups which may result in dissent, the state hoped to quell any desire to split away by defining these groups and giving them special status and privileges granted only to those with ethnic minority status.

Today, nearly 100 million people within China are considered an "ethnic minority," constituting roughly 8 percent of the population. The various ethnic minorities of China, other than sharing their identity as such, have little in common. They are as diverse and distinct as one nation's people to the next, speaking different languages, practicing different religions with totally separate histories and ancestral lines. There are five separate Autonomous Regions within China, whose ethnic minorities dominate the population of their respective region: Tibet, Inner Mongolia, and the Xinjiang-Uighur, Guangxi-Zhuang, and Ningxia-Hui Autonomous Regions. The Zhuang, Hui, and Uighur ethnic minorities make up the three largest minority populations in China, with populations

Left: *The majestic Snow Mountain sits just outside the ancient city of Lijiang in Yunnan province.*

Right: *The northern and northeastern regions of China suffer severe winters.*

of 15.5 million, 9.8 million and 8 million respectively. The Tibetan population is estimated at 4.5 million, although exact population numbers of Tibetans, along with the many other ethnic minority populations, are disputed.

Each ethnic minority within China is distinct. Though some share commonalities with other ethnic minorities or with the Han majority, most ethnic minorities vary immensely from one another. In the southwest provinces of Yunnan, Sichuan, and Guizhou can the most ethnic groups be found, making it the most diverse region in all of China. More than 20 distinct minority groups live in this area, including the Naxi and Bai of Yunnan, and the Dai and Hani of the Xishuangbanna region that borders Vietnam and Laos. The northwest is home to the Uighur of Xinjiang and Tibetans, who are native to not only the Tibetan Autonomous Region, but to the provinces of Sichuan and Qinghai as well. Other groups that occupy this area include the Hui, Kazakhs, Uzbeks, and Mongols. The Miao, Dong, Yao and Zhuang people of southern China constitute the largest group of ethnic minorities in the country. And the northeast is home to China's smallest group, the Oroqen, who live primarily in Inner Mongolia.

While the history of China is also a history of its ethnic minorities, it is primarily the history of the Han Chinese. To be considered "Han" is equivalent to being considered "Chinese." It is common for someone to refer to themselves as "Han" before they would call themselves "Chinese." For centuries, a notion of what it means to be Chinese has been constructed along ancestral lines. The tenets of filial piety have, since Confucius' time, tied the living to one's past through

Left: *The ethnic customs of China's numerous minority cultures are put on display in many Chinese cities. They attract tourists to many of the autonomous regions within China.*

Above: *The Qinghai Tibetan grasslands are home to many nomadic groups, who subsist by grazing animals, such as sheep and yak.*

Above: *A fisherman's boat on Er Hai Lake in Dali, Yunnan.*

Right: *A typical mountain house in western China.*

ancestral lines, reinforcing a notion of an ethnic Chinese-ness. The importance of both ancestry and filial piety within China has perhaps played a larger role in what it means to be Chinese than stereotypical cultural markers, like *guanxi* or saving face, have. For many, both living in China and outside of China, being Chinese is equated to ancestral ties and bloodlines. Considering themselves "descendants of the dragon," the Chinese people look to ancestry for their identity and sense of belonging.

Early legends of the dragon in Chinese lore describe a total of nine types of dragons that exist in the world. Of these nine, there are four types of this mythical animal that reappear again and again in Chinese beliefs. These four types of dragons live in different worlds, each having its own universe to guard, each with a symbology of its own. The first group of dragons, *tian long*, are those dragons that encompass the power of the heavens and have specific regenerative qualities. The second group are those who belong to the spirit world—the *shen long*—and are said to control the rain. The earth dragons are the *di long* who see to the waterways of earth. The last group are the dragons who guard over treasure, the *fu cang long*. The number four is also associated with the four directions of the earth, which play a pivotal role in *feng shui*. The mythical Emperor Fuxi, who could take the shape of a dragon, it was believed, governed each direction. The Dragon King, as he became known, guards over the dragons of the east, west, north and south as well as the water that covers the earth. Within Daoism, the dragon symbolized the way, or the *dao*: the force that guides all of life on earth and throughout the universe. In *feng shui*, the ideal location for a residence is called the "dragon's head" and once the

home is completed, the owners offer their new abode to come and live with them in an area designated for him. At this time, special offerings are made in the shape of a dragon in the hope that this great and powerful beast will confer harmony and happiness over their new dwelling.

Dragons recur again and again in China's history and identity as a people. The dragon is a symbol of their past, of their home, of their country and of their unity. To be a descendant of the dragon is to be part of this country that is as dynamic, vibrant, and transformative as the mythical creature it symbolizes.

Left: *Spectacular autumn leaves at Er Hai Lake.*

Below: *The climate of China is diverse; however, many regions experience four distinct seasons.*

Within Daoism, the dragon symbolized the way, or the dao: *the force that guides all of life on earth and throughout the universe... To be a descendant of the dragon is to be part of a country that is as dynamic, vibrant, and transformative as the mythical creature it symbolizes.*

Above: *The bicycle is still the main mode of transportation for the many citizens of Beijing.*

Below: *Workers sit beside the distinctive ruddy walls of the Forbidden City.*

Useful Information

China: Facts and Figures

Unless otherwise noted, all figures are based on July 2006 statistics.

People

Population:
Approx. 1.3 billion

Sex Ratio:
at birth: 1.12 male(s)/female
under 15 years: 1.13 male(s)/female
15-64 years: 1.06 male(s)/female
65 years and over: 0.91 male(s)/female
total population: 1.06 male(s)/female

Life Expectancy at Birth:
total population: 72.58 years
male: 70.89 years
female: 74.46 years

Median age:
total: 32.7 years
male: 32.3 years
female: 33.2 years

Land

Area:
total: 3,705,407 sq mi
land: 3,600,947 sq mi
water: 104,460 sq mi

Land Boundaries:
Afghanistan, Bhutan, Burma, India, Kazakhstan, North Korea, Kyrgyzstan, Laos, Mongolia, Nepal, Pakistan, Russia, Tajikistan, Vietnam

Water Boundaries:
East China Sea, Korea Bay, Yellow Sea, South China Sea

Administrative divisions:
23 provinces, 5 autonomous regions, and 4 municipalities

Provinces:
Anhui, Fujian, Gansu, Guangdong, Guizhou, Hainan, Hebei, Heilongjiang, Henan, Hubei, Hunan, Jiangsu, Jiangxi, Jilin, Liaoning, Qinghai, Shaanxi, Shandong, Shanxi, Sichuan, Yunnan, Zhejiang

Autonomous regions:
Guangxi, Inner Mongolia, Ningxia, Tibet, Xinjiang

Municipalities:
Beijing, Chongqing, Shanghai, Tianjin

Language:

a note on pronunciation

The most widely used system of spelling standard Mandarin Chinese today is referred to as the Pinyin system. Mandarin Chinese contains a total of four tones: a flat tone (ā), a rising tone (á), a falling-rising tone (ǎ), and a falling tone (à). Pronunciation of some letters in Pinyin differs somewhat from English pronunciation, especially with certain consonants. The following is a rough guide on how to pronounce some of the words used in this book.

c   pronounced **ts**
shucai, meaning vegetable, is pronounced shoo-ts-eye

q   pronounced **ch**
the province Qinghai is pronounced ching-high

x   pronounced **sh**
the early capital of China, Xi'an, is pronounced shee-an

z   pronounced **ds**
zaijian, meaning goodbye, is pronounced ds-eye-jen

zh pronounced **j**
the Zhou dynasty is pronounced like the name "Joe"

Sources of Further Information

China National Tourist Office
Website: www.cnto.org

New York office:
350 Fifth Avenue, Suite 6413
Empire State Building
New York, NY 10118
Phone: 1-888-760-8218

Los Angeles office:
550 North Brand Blvd., Suite 910
Glendale, CA 91203
Phone: 1-800-670-2228

2008 Beijing Olympics
http://en.beijing2008.cn/
The official website of the Beijing
2008 Summer Olympic Games

China Culture
www.chinaculture.org
Maintained by the Chinese
Ministry of Culture, this site
contains a wealth of information
about traditional and modern
Chinese art and culture, as well as
events and museums.

China Daily
www.chinadaily.com.cn
A news portal giving access
to stories from all over China.
Includes web TV clips and
slide shows.

South China Morning Post
www.scmp.com
The online edition of Hong
Kong's leading English-language
newspaper.

People's Daily Online
english.people.com.cn
The English-language edition
of the People's Daily, which is
China's largest-circulation daily
newspaper, with official news from
the government of the PRC.

ExpatsInChina
www.expatsinchina.com
A site with practical information
by and for Westerners living in
China.

**The Chinese Culture Center of
San Francisco**
www.c-c-c.org
This is a non-profit organization
based near San Francisco's famous
Chinatown that aims to increase
awareness of Chinese art and
culture in the US.

Index

References with images are in **bold**.